THE COMPLETE
CHINESE
COOKBOOK

THE COMPLETE
CHINESE
COOKBOOK

TORMONT

Contents

Photography by Peter Barry and Jean-Paul Paireault
Designed by Sally Strugnell
Jacket Design by Zapp
Typesetting by Julie Smith
Edited by Jillian Stewart
Recipes by Lalita Ahmed, Carolyn Garner,
Moyra Frazer, Judith Ferguson and Frederic Lebain

This edition published in 1993 by Tormont Publications Inc.
338 Saint Antoine St. East, Montreal, Canada H2Y 1A3
Tel. (514) 954-1441   Fax (514) 954-1443.

ISBN 2-89429-195-7
Printed in Canada

Introduction

As in any other style of cooking, Chinese food is a symbol of life and good health, forming a central part of family and social activity for many people. To the Chinese family, a meal is therefore about much more that just satisfying a physical need, it is an integral part of their social life.

In Chinese cuisine, the preparation of the food is of paramount importance. Many dishes require very fine chopping and shredding of the various ingredients, and they are combined in a very orderly manner. Those ingredients which are not available in the Western world can be substituted with similar products and alternatives to foods which may be difficult to obtain are given in the recipes. It is not necessary to use only Chinese utensils as many dishes can easily be prepared using basic kitchen equipment.

The main cooking technique used to produce Chinese food is stir frying. A wok is ideal, but a deep non-stick pan will serve the purpose. Stir-frying requires good temperature control and this is easily learnt through practice. The wok should be heated, then the temperature reduced before adding the cooking oil. If the utensil is too hot the oil will burn, giving a charred, oily taste to the food. The heat should be progressively raised for the addition of other ingredients. The whole process may take between five and seven minutes. The most important thing to remember is to never overcook, as this will not only destroy the crispness of the food, but also its flavor and goodness.

Chinese food incorporates six basic flavors: sweet, sour, salty, spicy, pungent and hot. Their employment and respective proportions must be well balanced. Flavoring is always supplemented by ready-made sauces, the most essential of which is soy sauce.

Finally, garnishing should not be neglected, as presentation is as important as preparation. After all, what appeals to the eye also appeals to the mind and stomach! A slice of cleverly carved carrot, a thin sliver of tomato and carefully arranged Chinese parsley can add that all important dash of color.

Cooking is always a pleasure, especially Chinese cooking. It is a challenge and a way to explore one's creative talents. In any case, who does not want their efforts rewarded by the pleasure of an exquisite Chinese meal.

Soups

Peking-Style Soup
Turkey Soup with Black Mushrooms
Eggflower Soup
Crab Soup with Ginger
Chicken Noodle Soup
Bamboo Shoot Soup
Chicken and Mushroom Soup
Wonton Soup
Duck Soup
Corn and Chicken Soup
Hot and Sour Soup
Crab and Watercress Soup
Noodles in Soup
Chinese Parsley and Fish Soup
Crab and Corn Soup

PEKING-STYLE SOUP

*Duck stock is the basis of this tasty, filling soup, which
contains meat and vegetables, and is delicately
flavored with sesame seeds and soy sauce.*

SERVES 4

4 slices smoked ham
1 head Chinese cabbage
3¾ cups duck stock
1 tbsp sesame seeds
Pinch chopped garlic
1 tbsp soy sauce
½ tsp white wine vinegar
Salt and pepper
1 egg yolk, beaten

1. Cut the ham into small, even-sized cubes.

2. Cut the Chinese cabbage into small pieces and simmer briskly for 10 minutes in the duck stock.

3. Stir in the sesame seeds, garlic, ham, soy sauce, vinegar and salt and pepper to taste.

4. Cook for 10 minute over a gentle heat. Using a teaspoon, drizzle the beaten egg yolk into the soup. Serve immediately.

TIME: Preparation takes about 5 minutes and cooking takes approximately 20 minutes.

VARIATION: Replace the smoked ham with a different smoked meat.

WATCHPOINT: The smoked ham is likely to change color during cooking.

TURKEY SOUP WITH BLACK MUSHROOMS

An unusual blend of flavors which makes a tasty, warming soup.

SERVES 4

6oz turkey breast meat
1 tbsp sesame oil
2oz dried Chinese black mushrooms,
   soaked for 15 minutes in warm water
3¾ cups chicken stock
1 tbsp soy sauce
1 slice fresh root ginger
Salt and pepper

1. Cut the turkey meat into thick slices and then into small cubes.

2. Heat the sesame oil in a wok and stir-fry the meat until brown. Remove from the pan and drain off any excess oil.

3. Cook the mushrooms in boiling, salted water for 10 minutes. Rinse and drain well.

4. Place the mushrooms in a saucepan with the stock. Stir in the meat, soy sauce, ginger, and salt and pepper to taste.

5. Bring to the boil and then simmer gently for 15 minutes.

6. Remove the slices of ginger just before serving. Serve the soup very hot.

TIME: Preparation takes about 8 minutes and cooking takes approximately 35 minutes.

SERVING IDEA: Sprinkle the soup with 1 tbsp chopped fresh chives before serving.

WATCHPOINT: Don't forget to remove the slice of ginger before serving.

EGGFLOWER SOUP

*The exotic name of this soup is derived from the
appearance of the egg in the soup.*

SERVES 4

14oz can plum tomatoes
1 tbsp light soy sauce
2½ cups chicken stock
2 eggs, lightly beaten
2 green onions, chopped finely

1. Drain and chop tomatoes, removing pips, and reserve juice.

2. Bring soy sauce, tomato juice and stock to the boil in the wok. Add tomatoes and half the green onions, and cook for 2 minutes.

3. Pour beaten eggs in gradually, stirring continuously.

4. Serve immediately, sprinkled with remaining green onions.

TIME: Preparation takes 10 minutes, cooking takes 10 minutes.

CRAB SOUP WITH GINGER

*This delicately flavored soup, with fresh crab and a
hint of ginger, is perfect for serving at a special dinner.*

SERVES 4

1 carrot, chopped
1 onion, chopped
½ leek, chopped
1 bay leaf
2 medium-sized crabs
3¾ cups fish stock
1-inch piece of fresh ginger root, chopped
1 tsp Sake Chinese wine (optional)
Salt and pepper

1. Make a vegetable stock by putting the carrot, onion, leek and bay leaf into a saucepan with a large quantity of water. Bring to the boil and add the crabs. Allow to boil briskly for 20 minutes or until cooked.

2. Remove the crabs when cooked and allow to cool. Once cooled, break off the pincers and break the joints, cut open the back and open the claws. Carefully remove all the crab meat.

3. Bring the fish stock to the boil and add the ginger, Sake and the crab meat. Boil for 15 minutes.

4. Check the seasoning, adding salt and pepper as necessary. Serve very hot.

TIME: Preparation takes about 40 minutes and cooking takes approximately 35 minutes. It takes about 30 minutes for the crab to cool, before you can comfortably remove the meat with your fingers.

WATCHPOINT: Allow plenty of time for opening the crab and removing all the meat. If time does not permit preparing fresh crab, use canned crab meat.

COOK'S TIP: Prepare the soup the day before serving. If allowed to rest overnight, the flavor of the soup will develop deliciously. Reheat gently just before serving.

CHICKEN NOODLE SOUP

A warming soup enhanced by filling noodles.

SERVES 4-6

1lb Shanghai noodles, or very thin noodles
2 tbsps oil
8oz cooked chicken, cubed
6oz Chinese white cabbage or ordinary white cabbage, shredded
6 cups chicken stock

Seasoning
½ tsp sugar
½ tsp salt
2 tsps Shao Hsing wine or dry sherry (optional)
½ tsp monosodium glutamate
2 tsps light soy sauce

1. Add the noodles to a large pan of boiling water. Stir to loosen the bundles and boil for 4-5 minutes. (The noodles should be just tender but not overcooked.) Drain noodles well.

2. Meanwhile, heat the oil in the wok and fry the chicken for 1-2 minutes. Remove the chicken and then fry the cabbage in the same oil for 2 minutes.

3. Add the seasoning ingredients and stir fry for 1 minute. Add the chicken and cook for a further 1-2 minutes until the cabbage is tender. Add the stock and bring to the boil.

4. Divide noodles among 6-8 warm soup bowls and add the hot soup. Serve immediately.

TIME: Preparation takes 10 minutes, cooking takes 10-12 minutes.

COOK'S TIP: Monosodium glutamate just adds that little bit of extra "bite" to the flavor of a dish.

BAMBOO SHOOT SOUP

A very decorative soup. Beaten egg sifted into the hot soup gives a very special effect.

SERVES 4

3oz bamboo shoots, cut into thin matchsticks
4 dried Chinese black mushrooms, soaked for 15 minutes in warm water
3¾ cups chicken stock
1 tbsp wine vinegar
2 tbsps light soy sauce
Salt and pepper
½ tsp cornstarch, combined with a little water
1 egg
10 chives

1. Blanch the bamboo shoots in boiling, salted water for 3 minutes. Rinse and set aside to drain.

2. Cook the mushrooms in boiling, salted water for 10 minutes. Rinse and set aside to drain.

3. Bring the stock to the boil and add the bamboo shoots, mushrooms, vinegar, and soy sauce, and season with salt and pepper to taste. Cook for 10 minutes.

4. Stir in the cornstarch and bring the soup slowly back to the boil.

5. Reduce the heat. Beat the egg thoroughly. Place the beaten egg in a strainer and add to the soup by shaking back and forth over the hot soup.

6. Add the chives to the soup and serve piping hot.

TIME: Preparation takes about 5 minutes and cooking takes approximately 30 minutes.

WATCHPOINT: Make sure the soup is boiling hot before adding the beaten egg.

COOK'S TIP: Try to buy fresh chives for this soup, as they have a much better flavor than dried chives.

CHICKEN AND MUSHROOM SOUP

A classic combination which works well.

SERVES 4

1 cup button mushrooms, sliced
½ cup dried brown mushrooms, soaked
  and then sliced
½ cup dried black mushrooms, soaked
  and then sliced
1 tbsp oil
6 cups chicken stock
1 cup shredded cooked chicken
3 green onions, finely chopped
¼ tsp monosodium glutamate (optional)
Salt to taste
1 tbsp light soy sauce
2 tsps Shao Hsing wine or dry sherry
  (optional)
Pinch ground white pepper
1 tsp cornstarch or arrowroot blended
  with 1 tbsp stock

1. Stir-fry the mushrooms in the oil for 2 minutes and then remove them.

2. Bring the stock to the boil in a large pan with the remaining ingredients, apart from the cornstarch and mushrooms.

3. Add the blended cornstarch and the mushrooms, and simmer for 1-2 minutes. Serve immediately.

TIME: Preparation takes 20 minutes, cooking takes 6-8 minutes.

COOK'S TIP: It is well worth hunting for the dried mushrooms as they taste wonderful. They are available in health food stores and Chinese supermarkets.

WONTON SOUP

Probably the best-known Chinese soup, this recipe uses
pre-made wonton wrappers for ease of preparation.

SERVES 6-8

20-24 wonton wrappers
½ cup finely ground chicken or pork
2 tbsps chopped Chinese parsley
    (cilantro)
3 green onions, finely chopped
1-inch piece fresh ginger, peeled
    and grated
1 egg, lightly beaten
6 cups chicken stock
1 tbsp dark soy sauce
Dash sesame oil
Salt and pepper
Chinese parsley or watercress for garnish

1. Place all the wonton wrappers on a
large, flat surface. Mix together the
chicken or pork, chopped parsley, green
onions and ginger. Brush the edges of the
wrappers lightly with beaten egg.

2. Place a small mound of mixture on one
half of the wrappers and fold the other
half over the top to form a triangle.

3. Press with the fingers to seal the edges
well.

4. Bring the stock to the boil in a large
saucepan. Add the filled wontons and
simmer 5-10 minutes or until they float to
the surface.

5. Add remaining ingredients to the soup,
using only the leaves of the parsley or
watercress for garnish.

TIME: Preparation takes 25-30 minutes, cooking takes about 5-10 minutes.

VARIATION: Use equal quantities of crabmeat or shrimp to fill the wontons
instead of chicken or pork.

BUYING GUIDE: Wonton wrappers are sometimes called wonton skins. They
are available in specialty shops, delicatessens and Chinese supermarkets.

DUCK SOUP

The perfect start to a Chinese meal,
and it doesn't take too long either.

SERVES 4

2 green onions, finely chopped
1 tbsp cooked oil
1-inch fresh root ginger, peeled and
  finely chopped
4oz cooked duck meat, chopped
4oz winter melon, thinly sliced
6 cups chicken stock
Salt to taste
Pinch monosodium glutamate (optional)
1 tbsp Shao Hsing wine or dry sherry
  (optional)
1 tsp arrowroot or cornstarch blended
  with 1 tbsp stock
Freshly ground black pepper to taste

1. Fry green onions in the oil for 1 minute.

2. Add ginger and duck meat. Stir-fry for 1 minute.

3. Add winter melon and stir-fry for a further 1-2 minutes and then add stock and the remaining ingredients.

4. Gently simmer for 2-3 minutes until the soup becomes clear. Serve immediately.

TIME: Preparation takes 10 minutes, cooking takes 8 minutes.

COOK'S TIP: Use the leftovers from a recipe such as Peking Duck for the meat in this recipe.

CORN AND CHICKEN SOUP

A classic soup which is still a great favorite.

SERVES 4

1 chicken, with giblets
8oz can creamy corn
1 onion, peeled and chopped roughly
1 carrot, scraped and chopped roughly
1 stick celery, chopped
6 peppercorns
Parsley stalks
1 bay leaf
1 quart water
Salt
Pepper

Garnish
Chopped parsley or chives

1. Clean chicken, and cut into quarters. Put into wok with giblets, chopped vegetables, peppercorns, bay leaf, parsley stalks, seasoning and water.

2. Bring to the boil. Reduce heat and simmer for 30 minutes. Strain and return stock to wok.

3. Discard the vegetables and giblets. Remove meat from chicken and cut into fine shreds.

4. Add undrained corn to stock, and bring to boil. Simmer for 5 minutes.

5. Add chicken and cook for 1 minute.

6. Sprinkle with chopped parsley or chives. Serve hot.

TIME: Preparation takes 15 minutes, cooking takes 45 minutes.

HOT AND SOUR SOUP

*A very warming soup, this is a favorite
in winter in Peking. Add chili sauce
and vinegar to suit your taste.*

SERVES 4-6

2oz pork
3 dried Chinese mushrooms, soaked in
  boiling water for 5 minutes and
  chopped
½ cup peeled, uncooked shrimp
6 cups chicken stock
1oz bamboo shoots, sliced
3 green onions, shredded
Salt and pepper
1 tbsp sugar
1 tsp dark soy sauce
½ tsp light soy sauce
1-2 tsps chili sauce
1½ tbsps vinegar
Dash sesame seed oil and rice wine or
  sherry
1 egg, well beaten
2 tbsps water mixed with 1 tbsp
  cornstarch

1. Trim any fat from the pork and slice it
into shreds about 2 inches long and less
than ½-inch thick.

2. Soak the mushrooms in boiling water
until softened. Place the pork in a large
pot with the shrimp and stock. Bring to
the boil and then reduce the heat to allow
to simmer gently for 4-5 minutes. Add all
the remaining ingredients except for the
egg, and cornstarch and water mixture.
Cook a further 1-2 minutes over low heat.

3. Remove the pan from the heat and add
the egg gradually, stirring gently until it
forms threads in the soup.

4. Mix a spoonful of the hot soup with the
cornstarch and water mixture and add to
the soup, stirring constantly.

5. Bring the soup back to simmering point
for 1 minute to thicken the cornstarch.
Serve immediately.

TIME: Preparation takes about 25 minutes, cooking takes 7-8 minutes.

PREPARATION: Vary the amount of chili sauce to suit your own taste.

VARIATION: Hot and Sour Soup is very versatile. Substitute other ingredients such as
chicken, crabmeat, bean sprouts, spinach or green cabbage.

WATCHPOINT: The soup must be hot enough to cook the egg when it is added, but not so
hot that the egg sets immediately.

CRAB AND WATERCRESS SOUP

Crab and watercress make a great combination in this quick soup.

SERVES 4-6

6 cups chicken stock
4oz white crab meat, shredded
2 green onions, finely chopped
2 bunches watercress, finely chopped
Salt and freshly ground black pepper to
    taste
1 tsp cornstarch or arrowroot
1 tbsp water
2 tsps light soy sauce
A few drops sesame oil

1. Bring the stock to the boil with the crab meat, onions and watercress and simmer for 4-5 minutes. Add salt and pepper to taste.

2. Mix the cornstarch with the water and add to the soup. Allow to simmer for a further 2 minutes.

3. Add soy sauce and sesame oil, mix well and simmer for 2 minutes. Serve immediately.

TIME: Preparation takes 10 minutes, cooking takes 8-9 minutes.

BUYING GUIDE: Ensure the watercress is not limp – it deteriorates rapidly once it reaches the supermarket.

NOODLES IN SOUP

A simple soup which is extremely tasty.

SERVES 4-6

1lb small rounds of noodle cakes
Salt
6 cups chicken or beef broth, or
   thick stock
4oz cooked shredded chicken
2 eggs, hard-cooked and sliced
4oz Chinese napa cabbage, finely
   shredded (or iceberg lettuce)
2 green onions, thinly sliced

1. Cook the noodles in boiling, salted water for 5 minutes. Drain thoroughly.

2. Heat the broth or stock and add salt to taste. Serve the cooked noodles in bowls, and pour over the hot broth.

3. Garnish with chicken, sliced eggs, cabbage and green onions, and serve.

TIME: Preparation takes 10 minutes, cooking takes 6-8 minutes.

BUYING GUIDE: Noodles are available in different thicknesses – buy the thinnest for soups.

CHINESE PARSLEY AND FISH SOUP

Chinese parsley is just another name for cilantro,
which is available in most supermarkets.

SERVES 4

1lb white fish fillet, cut into 6 even-
   sized pieces
4 cups chicken stock
½-inch fresh root ginger, peeled and
   thinly sliced
Salt to taste
Freshly ground black pepper to taste
Pinch monosodium glutamate (optional)
2 green onions, finely chopped
½ tsp arrowroot or cornstarch
2 sprigs Chinese parsley, finely chopped
18-20 thin cucumber slices

1. Wash fish in cold water and gently simmer in chicken stock for 2-3 minutes. Remove the fish pieces carefully.

2. Add ginger, salt, pepper, monosodium glutamate and green onion, and simmer the stock for 2-3 minutes. Strain.

3. Dissolve arrowroot in 1 tbsp water or cold stock and add to the soup. Simmer for 2 minutes until the soup thickens.

4. Add fish pieces and bring back to the boil. Serve in soup bowls, sprinkled with chopped parsley and cucumber slices.

TIME: Preparation takes 10 minutes, cooking takes 7-8 minutes.

COOK'S TIP: Use your favorite white fish for this recipe.

CRAB AND CORN SOUP

*Creamed corn and succulent crabmeat
combine to make a velvety rich soup. Whisked
egg whites add an interesting texture.*

SERVES 4-6

4 cups chicken or fish stock
12oz creamed corn
4oz crabmeat
Salt and pepper
1 tsp light soy sauce
2 tbsps cornstarch
3 tbsps water or stock
2 egg whites, whisked
4 green onions for garnish

1. Bring the stock to the boil in a large pan. Add the corn, crabmeat, seasoning and soy sauce. Allow to simmer for 4-5 minutes.

2. Mix the cornstarch and water or stock and add a spoonful of the hot soup. Return the mixture to the soup and bring back to the boil. Cook until the soup thickens.

3. Whisk the egg whites until soft peaks form. Stir into the hot soup just before serving.

4. Slice the onions thinly on the diagonal and scatter over the top to serve.

TIME: Preparation takes about 10 minutes, cooking takes about 8-10 minutes.

PREPARATION: Adding the egg whites is optional.

WATCHPOINT: Do not allow the corn and the crab to boil rapidly; they will both toughen.

ECONOMY: Use crab sticks instead of crabmeat.

VARIATION: Chicken may be used instead of the crabmeat and the cooking time increased to 10-12 minutes.

Snacks and Appetizers

Quick-Fried Shrimp
Pot Sticker Dumplings
The Peking Duck
Rice Paper Shrimp Parcels
Cantonese Egg Fu Yung
Barbecued Spare Ribs
Shrimp Fu Yung
Sesame Chicken Wings
Noodles with Ginger and Oyster Sauce
Spring Rolls
Szechuan Bang Bang Chicken
Shanghai Noodles
Steamed Cabbage Rolls with
Fish and Crabmeat
Snow Peas with Shrimp

QUICK-FRIED SHRIMP

*Prepared with either raw or cooked shrimp, this is
an incredibly delicious appetizer that is extremely easy to cook.*

SERVES 4-6

2lbs cooked shrimp in their shells
2 cloves garlic, crushed
1-inch piece fresh ginger, finely
    chopped
1 tbsp chopped fresh Chinese parsley
    (cilantro)
3 tbsps oil
1 tbsp rice wine or dry sherry
1½ tbsps light soy sauce
Chopped green onions to garnish

1. Shell the shrimp except for the very tail
ends. Place the shrimp in a bowl with the
remaining ingredients, except for the
garnish, and leave to marinate for 30
minutes.

2. Heat a wok and add the shrimp and
their marinade. Stir-fry briefly to heat the
shrimp.

3. Chop the onions roughly or cut into
neat rounds. Sprinkle over the shrimp to
serve.

TIME: Preparation takes about 30 minutes for the shrimp to marinate.
Cooking takes about 2 minutes.

WATCHPOINT: Do not overcook the shrimp as they will toughen.

VARIATION: If uncooked shrimp are available, stir-fry with their marinade
until they turn pink.

POT STICKER DUMPLINGS

*So called because they are fried in very little oil,
they will stick unless they are brown and crisp
on the bottom before they are steamed.*

MAKES 12

Dumplings
1½ cups all-purpose flour
½ tsp salt
3 tbsps oil
Boiling water

Filling
¾ cup finely ground pork or chicken
4 water chestnuts, finely chopped
3 green onions, finely chopped
½ tsp five spice powder
1 tbsp light soy sauce
1 tsp sugar
1 tsp sesame oil

1. Sift the flour and salt into a large bowl and make a well in the center. Pour in the oil and add enough boiling water to make a pliable dough. Add about 4 tbsps water at first and begin stirring with a wooden spoon to gradually incorporate the flour. Add more water as necessary. Knead the dough for about 5 minutes and allow to rest for 30 minutes.

2. Divide the dough into 12 pieces and roll each piece out to a circle about 6 inches in diameter.

3. Mix all the filling ingredients together and place a mound of filling on half of each circle. Fold over the top and press the edges together firmly. Roll over the joined edges using a twisting motion and press down to seal.

4. Pour about ⅛ inch of oil in a large frying pan, preferably cast iron. When the oil is hot, add the dumplings flat side down and cook until nicely browned.

5. When the underside is brown, add about 3 fl oz water to the pan and cover it tightly.

6. Continue cooking gently for about 5 minutes, or until the top surface of dumplings is steamed and appears cooked. Serve immediately.

TIME: Preparation takes about 50 minutes including the standing time for the dough. Cooking takes about 10-20 minutes.

PREPARATION: The pan used for cooking must have a flat base. Do not use a wok.

WATCHPOINT: Make sure the dumplings are brown and crisp on the bottom before adding the water otherwise they really will be pot stickers!

THE PEKING DUCK

A magnificent recipe much loved by all fans of Chinese cooking.

SERVES 6

1 duck, weighing 4lbs
½ medium cucumber
4 green onions

Sauce
Small can yellow bean sauce
3 tbsps sugar
2 tbsps oil

1. Clean and dry the duck. Leave in a cool place overnight.

2. Finely shred the cucumber and green onions.

3. Preheat the oven to 400°F. Place the duck on a grill rack set on top of a baking pan. Cook the duck for 1¼ hours. The duck should be very dark and crispy.

4. For the sauce, heat 2 tbsps oil in a small pan. Add the yellow bean paste and sugar. Cook together for 1-2 minutes.

5. Peel the skin off the duck and cut into 2-inch slices. Serve on a heated platter. Carve the meat off the duck into 2-inch slices, serve on a separate platter.

6. The duck skin and meat are eaten by wrapping them in pancakes which are first of all brushed with a teaspoon of duck sauce and a layer of cucumber and green onions.

TIME: Preparation takes about 15 minutes, cooking takes nearly 2 hours.

RICE PAPER SHRIMP PARCELS

The perfect nibble for a cocktail party.

MAKES ABOUT 20 PARCELS

8oz shrimp, shelled and de-veined
1 egg white
½ tsp cornstarch
1 tsp Chinese wine, or 2 tsps dry sherry
1 tsp sugar
1 tsp light soy sauce
6 green onions, finely sliced
Salt
Pepper
⅔ cup peanut oil
1 packet rice paper

1. Dry the prepared shrimp on paper towels.

2. Mix egg white, cornstarch, wine, sugar, soy sauce, green onions and seasoning together. Mix in shrimp.

3. Heat peanut oil in wok until hot.

4. Wrap five or six shrimp in each piece of rice paper.

5. Gently drop in rice paper parcels and deep-fry for about 5 minutes. Serve hot.

TIME: Preparation takes 15 minutes, cooking takes 15 minutes.

CANTONESE EGG FU YUNG

*As the name suggests, this dish is from Canton.
However, fu yung dishes are popular in
many other regions of China, too.*

SERVES 2-3

5 eggs
½ cup shredded cooked meat, poultry
    or fish
1 stick celery, finely shredded
4 Chinese dried mushrooms, soaked in
    boiling water for 5 minutes
1 cup bean sprouts
1 small onion, thinly sliced
Pinch salt and pepper
1 tsp dry sherry
Oil for frying

Sauce
1 tbsp cornstarch dissolved in 3 tbsps
    cold water
1¼ cups chicken stock
1 tsp tomato catsup
1 tbsp soy sauce
Pinch salt and pepper
Dash sesame oil

1. Beat the eggs lightly and add the
shredded meat and celery.

2. Squeeze all the liquid from the dried
mushrooms. Remove the stems and cut
the caps into thin slices. Add the egg
mixture along with the bean sprouts and
onion. Add a pinch of salt and pepper and
the sherry and stir well.

3. Heat a wok or frying pan and pour in
about 4 tbsps oil. When hot, carefully
spoon in about 5 tbsps of the egg mixture.

4. Brown on one side, turn gently over
and brown the other side. Remove the
cooked patties to a plate and continue
until all the mixture is cooked.

5. Combine all the sauce ingredients in a
small, heavy-based pan and bring slowly
to the boil, stirring continuously until
thickened and cleared. Pour the sauce
over the Egg Fu Yung to serve.

TIME: Preparation takes 25 minutes, cooking takes about
5 minutes for the patties and 8 minutes for the sauce.

VARIATION: Use cooked shellfish such as crab or lobster,
if desired. Fresh mushrooms may be used instead of the dried ones.
Divide mixture in half or in thirds and cook one large patty per person.

ECONOMY: Left-over cooked meat such as beef, pork or chicken
can be used as an ingredient.

BARBECUED SPARE RIBS

*Although Chinese barbecue sauce is nothing like
the tomato-based American-style sauce, these ribs
are still tasty cooked on a grill.*

SERVES 6-8

4lbs fresh spare-ribs
¼ cup dark soy sauce
½ cup Hoisin sauce
3 tbsps dry sherry
¼ tsp five spice powder
1 tbsp brown sugar
4-6 green onions for garnish

1. First prepare the garnish. Trim the root ends and the dark green tops from the onions.

2. Cut both ends into thin strips, leaving about ½ inch in the middle uncut.

3. Place the onions in ice water for several hours or overnight for the ends to curl up.

4. Cut the spare-ribs into one-rib pieces. Mix all the remaining ingredients together, pour over the ribs and stir to coat evenly. Allow to stand for 1 hour.

5. Put the spare-rib pieces on a rack in a roasting pan containing 2½ cups water and cook in a preheated 350°F oven for 30 minutes. Add more hot water to the pan while cooking, if necessary.

6. Turn the ribs over and brush with the remaining sauce. Cook 30 minutes longer, or until tender. Serve garnished with the onion brushes.

TIME: Preparation takes about 45 minutes. The onion brushes must soak for at least 4 hours and the ribs must marinate for 1 hour. Cooking takes about 1 hour.

PREPARATION: If the ribs are small and not very meaty, cut into two-rib pieces before cooking, then into one-rib pieces just before serving.

COOK'S TIP: The ribs may be prepared in advance and reheated at the same temperature for about 10 minutes.

SHRIMP FU YUNG

This dish is perfect for lunch or an evening snack.

SERVES 4-6

Oil
1-2 cloves of garlic, chopped
4oz shrimp, peeled
4oz green beans, sliced
1 carrot, shredded
6 eggs
Salt and freshly ground black pepper to
    taste
1 cup chicken stock
¼ tsp salt
2 tsps soy sauce
1 tsp sugar
1 tsp cornstarch

1. Heat 2 tbsps oil in a wok. Add the garlic and stir-fry for 1 minute.

2. Add the shrimp and stir-fry for 1 minute.

3. Add the beans and carrots and stir-fry for 2 minutes. Remove and keep on one side.

4. Beat the eggs with salt and pepper to taste, and add the cooled shrimp mixture.

5. Clean the wok and heat 1 tsp oil. Pour 4 tbsps of the egg mixture and cook like a pancake. When the egg is set, turn the pancake over and cook on the other side until lightly golden. Place on a warm platter and keep warm.

6. To make the sauce beat the stock with the other sauce ingredients and stir over a gentle heat until the sauce thickens. Serve the pancakes with this sauce.

TIME: Preparation takes 10 minutes, cooking takes 4 minutes for filling and
3-4 minutes for each pancake.

SESAME CHICKEN WINGS

*This is an economical appetizer that is also good as a
cocktail snack or as a light meal with stir-fried vegetables.*

SERVES 8

12 chicken wings
1 tbsp salted black beans
1 tbsp water
1 tbsp oil
2 cloves garlic, crushed
2 slices fresh ginger, cut into fine shreds
4 tbsps soy sauce
2 tbsps dry sherry or rice wine
Large pinch black pepper
1 tbsp sesame seeds

1. Cut off and discard the wing tips. Cut between the joint to separate into twin pieces.

2. Crush the beans and add the water. Leave to stand.

3. Heat the oil in a wok and add the garlic and ginger. Stir briefly and add the chicken wings. Cook, stirring, until lightly browned, about 3 minutes. Add the soy sauce and wine and cook, stirring, about 30 seconds longer. Add the soaked black beans and pepper.

4. Cover the wok tightly and allow to simmer for about 8-10 minutes. Uncover and turn the heat to high. Continue cooking, stirring until the liquid is almost evaporated and the chicken wings are glazed with sauce.

5. Remove from the heat and sprinkle on sesame seeds. Stir to coat completely and serve. Garnish with green onions or Chinese parsley, if desired.

TIME: Preparation takes about 25 minutes, cooking takes about 13-14 minutes.

WATCHPOINT: Sesame seeds pop slightly as they cook.

COOK'S TIP: You can prepare the chicken wings ahead of time and reheat them. They are best reheated in the oven for about 5 minutes at 350°F.

SERVING IDEA: To garnish with green onion brushes, trim the roots and green tops off green onions and cut both ends into thin strips, leaving the middle intact. Place in ice water for several hours or overnight for the cut ends to curl up. Drain and use to garnish.

Noodles with Ginger and Oyster Sauce

*Noodles stir-fried with ginger, carrot and zucchini,
then served in an oyster sauce.*

SERVES 4

8oz Chinese noodles
1 carrot
1 zucchini
3 slices fresh ginger root
1 green onion, cut into thin rounds
1 tbsp oil
1 tbsp soy sauce
3 tbsps oyster sauce
Salt and pepper

1. Cook the noodles in boiling, salted water, rinse them under cold water, and set aside to drain.

2. Cut the carrot into thin strips. Thickly peel the zucchini to include a little of the flesh and cut into thin strips. Discard the center of the zucchini.

3. Peel the fresh ginger root sparingly, but remove any hard parts. Slice thinly, using a potato peeler. Cut the slices into thin strips, using a very sharp knife.

4. Heat the oil in a wok, and stir-fry the green onion for 10 seconds then add the carrot, zucchini and ginger, and stir-fry briefly.

5. Stir in the noodles and cook for 1 minute.

6. Stir in the soy and oyster sauces, and continue cooking until heated through. Season with salt and pepper and serve.

TIME: Preparation takes about 15 minutes and cooking takes approximately 15 minutes.

VARIATION: Cook the noodles in chicken stock instead of salted water to give them extra flavor.

COOK'S TIP: Stir-fry the ginger and the other vegetables very quickly, to avoid browning them. Lower the heat if necessary.

SPRING ROLLS

*One of the most popular Chinese hors d'oeuvres,
these are delicious dipped in sweet-sour sauce.*

MAKES 12

Wrappers
1 cup all-purpose flour
1 egg, beaten
Cold water

Filling
8oz pork, trimmed and finely shredded
4oz shrimp, shelled and chopped
4 green onions, finely chopped
2 tbsps chopped fresh ginger
4oz Chinese leaves, shredded
2 cups bean sprouts
1 tbsp light soy sauce
Dash sesame seed oil
1 egg, beaten

1. To prepare the wrappers, sift the flour into a bowl and make a well in the center. Add the beaten egg and about 1 tbsp cold water. Begin beating with a wooden spoon, gradually drawing in the flour from the outside to make a smooth dough. Add more water if necessary.

2. Knead the dough until it is elastic and pliable. Place in a covered bowl and chill for about 4 hours or overnight.

3. When ready to roll out, allow the dough to come back to room temperature. Flour a large work surface well and roll the dough out to about ¼-inch thick.

4. Cut the dough into 12 equal squares and then roll each piece into a larger square about 6 x 6 inches. The dough should be very thin. Cover while preparing the filling.

5. Cook the pork in a little of the frying oil for about 2-3 minutes. Add the remaining filling ingredients, except the beaten egg, cook for 2-3 minutes and allow to cool.

6. Lay out the wrappers on a clean work surface with the point of each wrapper facing you. Brush the edges lightly with the beaten egg.

7. Divide the filling among all twelve wrappers, placing it just above the front point. Fold over the sides like an envelope.

8. Fold over the point until the filling is completely covered. Roll up as for a jelly roll. Press all the edges to seal well.

9. Heat the oil in a deep fat fryer or in a deep pan to 375°F. Depending upon the size of the fryer, place in 2-4 spring rolls and fry until golden brown on both sides. The rolls will float to the surface when one side has browned and should then be turned over. Drain thoroughly on paper towels and serve hot.

TIME: Preparation takes about 50 minutes for the wrapper dough, the filling and for rolling up. Dough must be allowed to rest for at least 4 hours before use. Cooking takes about 20 minutes.

SZECHUAN BANG BANG CHICKEN

This is a good dish to serve as an appetizer.

SERVES 2

2 chicken breasts
1 medium cucumber

Sauce
5 tbsps peanut butter
2 tsps sesame oil
½ tsp sugar
¼ tsp salt
2 tsps stock
½ tsp chili sauce

1. Simmer the chicken in a pan of water for 30 minutes. Remove the chicken breasts and cut them into ½-inch thick strips.

2. Thinly slice the cucumber. Spread cucumber on a large serving platter. Pile the shredded chicken on top.

3. Mix the peanut butter with the sesame oil, sugar, salt and stock. Pour the sauce evenly over the chicken.

4. Sprinkle the chili sauce evenly over the top.

TIME: Cooking takes about 30 minutes, final preparation takes 5 minutes.

SHANGHAI NOODLES

In general, noodles are more popular in northern and eastern China, than in other parts of the country. Noodles make a popular snack in Chinese tea houses.

SERVES 4

3 tbsps oil
4oz chicken breast meat
1lb thick Shanghai noodles
4oz Chinese cabbage
4 green onions, thinly sliced
2 tbsps soy sauce
Freshly ground black pepper
Dash sesame oil

1. Heat the oil in the wok and add the chicken cut into thin shreds. Stir-fry for 2-3 minutes.

2. Meanwhile, cook the noodles in boiling salted water until just tender – about 6-8 minutes. Drain in a colander and rinse under hot water. Toss in the colander to drain and leave to dry.

3. Add the shredded Chinese cabbage and green onions to the chicken in the wok along with the soy sauce, pepper and sesame oil. Cook about 1 minute and toss in the cooked noodles. Stir well and heat through. Serve immediately.

TIME: Preparation takes about 10 minutes, cooking takes 6-8 minutes.

VARIATION: Pork may be used instead of the chicken. Add fresh spinach, shredded, if desired and cook with the Chinese cabbage.

BUYING GUIDE: Shanghai noodles are available in Chinese supermarkets and also some delicatessens. If unavailable, substitute tagliatelle or dried Chinese noodles.

STEAMED CABBAGE ROLLS WITH FISH AND CRABMEAT

*This dish can be served as an appetizer for four people
or as a main dish for two.*

SERVES 4

8 large Chinese cabbage leaves
½lb filleted white fish
2 slices ginger root
1½ tsps salt
1 egg white
1 tsp sesame oil
½lb crabmeat

1. Pour boiling water over the cabbage to soften. Drain and dry well.

2. Chop the fish coarsely. Finely chop the ginger. Place the fish and ginger in a bowl with the salt, egg white, sesame oil and crabmeat. Mix well.

3. Place 2 cabbage leaves on a flat surface. Put fish mixture into the center of each of the leaves. Roll the leaves up to form a tight roll.

4. Repeat until all the fish mixture has been used.

5. Insert the fish rolls into a steamer. Steam vigorously for 10-12 minutes. Place the cooked rolls on a heated platter and serve with soy sauce, and chili sauce as dips.

TIME: Preparation takes about 15 minutes, cooking takes 10-12 minutes.

BUYING GUIDE: If you cannot obtain fresh crabmeat use the canned variety.

SNOW PEAS WITH SHRIMP

*Snow peas, peapods and mange tout are all names for the same vegetable –
bright green, crisp and edible, pods and all.*

SERVES 2-4

3 tbsps oil
2oz split blanched almonds, halved
4oz snow peas
2 tsps cornstarch
2 tsps light soy sauce
1 cup chicken stock
2 tbsps dry sherry
Salt and pepper
2oz bamboo shoots, sliced
1lb cooked, peeled shrimp

1. Heat the oil in a wok. Add the almonds and cook over moderate heat until golden brown. Remove from the oil and drain on paper towels.

2. To prepare the snow peas, tear off the stems and pull them downwards to remove any strings. If the snow peas are small, just remove the stalks. Add the snow peas to the hot oil and cook for about 1 minute. Remove and set aside with the almonds.

3. Drain all the oil from the wok and mix together the cornstarch and the remaining ingredients, except the shrimp and bamboo shoots. Pour the mixture into the wok and stir constantly while bringing to the boil. Allow to simmer for 1-2 minutes until thickened and cleared.

4. Stir in the shrimp and all the other ingredients and heat through for about 1 minute. Serve immediately.

TIME: Preparation takes about 10 minutes, cooking takes 6-8 minutes.

VARIATION: If using green onions, celery or water chestnuts, cook with the snow peas.

WATCHPOINT: Do not cook the shrimp too long or on heat that is too high –
they toughen quite easily.

Fish and Seafood

Singapore Fish
Cantonese Shrimp
Szechuan Fish
Shrimp and Ginger
Shrimp in Hot Sauce
Sweet-Sour Fish
Steamed Shrimp
Shrimp with Broccoli
Szechuan Fish Steak
Crispy Fish with Chili
Seafood Chow Mein
Kung Pao Shrimp with Cashew Nuts

SINGAPORE FISH

*The cuisine of Singapore was much influenced by that of
China. In turn, the Chinese introduced ingredients
like curry powder into their cuisine.*

SERVES 4

1lb white fish fillets
1 egg white
1 tbsp cornstarch
2 tsps white wine
Salt and pepper
Oil for frying
1 large onion, cut into ½-inch
    thick wedges
1 tbsp mild curry powder
1 small can pineapple pieces, drained and
    juice reserved, or ½ fresh pineapple,
    peeled and cubed
1 small can mandarin orange segments,
    drained and juice reserved
1 small can sliced water chestnuts, drained
1 tbsp cornstarch mixed with juice of 1
    lime
2 tsps sugar (optional)
Pinch salt and pepper

1. Starting at the tail end of the fillets, skin
them using a sharp knife.

2. Slide the knife back and forth along the
length of each fillet, pushing the fish flesh
along as you go.

3. Cut the fish into even-sized pieces,
about 2 inches square.

4. Mix together the egg white, cornstarch,
wine, salt and pepper. Place the fish in the
mixture and leave to stand while heating
the oil.

5. When the oil is hot, fry a few pieces of
fish at a time until light golden brown and
crisp. Remove the fish to paper towels to
drain, and continue until all the fish is
cooked.

6. Remove all but 1 tbsp of the oil from
the wok and add the onion. Stir-fry the
onion for 1-2 minutes and add the curry
powder. Cook the onion and curry
powder for a further 1-2 minutes. Add the
juice from the pineapple and mandarin
oranges and bring to the boil.

7. Combine the cornstarch and lime juice
and add a spoonful of the boiling fruit
juice. Return the mixture to the wok and
cook until thickened, about 2 minutes.
Taste and add sugar if desired.

8. Add the fruit, water chestnuts and fried
fish to the wok and stir to coat. Heat
through 1 minute and serve immediately.

TIME: Preparation takes about 25 minutes, cooking takes about 10 minutes.

VARIATION: Chicken may be used in place of the fish and cooked in the same way.
Garnish with Chinese parsley leaves if desired.

SERVING IDEA: Serve with plain rice, fried rice or cooked Chinese noodles.

CANTONESE SHRIMP

*This quick and easy recipe is suitable for those
times when unexpected friends drop in for lunch.*

SERVES 2-3

3 tbsps oil
2 cloves garlic, finely crushed
1lb peeled shrimp
2 inch piece root ginger, peeled and finely
　chopped
4oz uncooked pork or bacon, finely
　chopped

Sauce
1 tbsp rice wine or dry sherry
1 tbsp light soy sauce
1 tsp sugar
1¼ cups stock or water
1 tbsp cornstarch mixed with
　2 tbsps stock or water

2-3 green onions, chopped
2 eggs, lightly beaten

1. Heat 1 tbsp oil in a wok. Add the garlic
and fry for 1 minute.

2. Add the shrimp and stir-fry for 4-5
minutes. Remove to a dish. Keep warm.

3. Add the remaining oil to the wok and
fry the ginger and pork for 3-4 minutes
until it loses its color.

4. Add the mixed sauce ingredients to the
wok and cook for 1 minute.

5. Add the onions and cook for 1 minute.
Add the beaten eggs and cook for 1-2
minutes, without stirring, until it sets.
Spoon the egg mixture over the shrimp.

6. Alternatively, add the shrimp along with
the beaten eggs. Allow the eggs to set and
then mix gently. Serve at once.

TIME: Preparation takes 10 minutes, cooking takes 15 minutes.

COOK'S TIP: Dry sherry is always a good substitute for Chinese wine so keep a bottle
specially for this purpose.

SZECHUAN FISH

The piquant spiciness of Szechuan pepper is quite different from that of black or white pepper. Beware, though, too much can numb the mouth temporarily!

SERVES 6

6 red or green chili peppers
1lb white fish fillets
Pinch salt and pepper
1 egg
6 tbsps flour
7 tbsps white wine
Oil for frying
2oz cooked ham, cut in small dice
1-inch piece fresh ginger, finely diced
½-1 red or green chili pepper, cored,
    seeded and finely diced
6 water chestnuts, finely diced
4 green onions, finely chopped
3 tbsps light soy sauce
1 tsp cider vinegar or rice wine vinegar
½ tsp ground Szechuan pepper
    (optional)
1¾ cups light stock
1 tbsp cornstarch dissolved with 2 tbsps
    water
2 tsps sugar

1. To prepare the garnish, choose unblemished chili peppers with the stems on. Using a small, sharp knife, cut peppers in strips, starting from the pointed end.

2. Cut down to within ½ inch of the stem end. Rinse out the seeds under cold running water and place the peppers in iced water.

3. Leave the peppers to soak for at least 4 hours or overnight until they open up like a flower.

4. Cut the fish fillets into 2-inch pieces and season with salt and pepper. Beat the egg well and add flour and wine to make a batter. Dredge the fish lightly with flour and then dip into the batter. Coat the fish well.

5. Heat a wok and when hot, add enough oil to deep-fry the fish. When the oil is hot, fry a few pieces of fish at a time, until golden brown. Drain and proceed until all the fish is cooked.

6. Remove all but 1 tbsp of oil from the wok and add the ham, ginger, diced chili pepper, water chestnuts and green onions. Cook for about 1 minute and add the soy sauce and vinegar. If using Szechuan pepper, add at this point. Stir well and cook for a further 1 minute. Remove the vegetables from the pan and set them aside.

7. Add the stock to the wok and bring to the boil. When boiling, add 1 spoonful of the hot stock to the cornstarch mixture. Add the mixture back to the stock and re-boil, stirring constantly until thickened.

8. Stir in the sugar and return the fish and vegetables to the sauce. Heat through for 30 seconds and serve at once.

TIME: Preparation takes about 30 minutes. Chili pepper garnish takes at least 4 hours to soak. Cooking takes about 10 minutes.

SHRIMP AND GINGER

An age-old combination which has stood the test of time.

SERVES 4

2 tbsps oil
1½lbs peeled shrimp
1 inch fresh root ginger, peeled and
   finely chopped
2 cloves garlic, peeled and finely chopped
2-3 green onions, chopped lengthways
   into 1-inch pieces
1 leek, white part only, cut into strips
¾ cup shelled peas
3 cups bean sprouts

Seasoning
2 tbsps dark soy sauce
1 tsp sugar
Pinch monosodium glutamate (optional)
Pinch of salt

1. Heat the oil in a wok and stir-fry the shrimp for 2-3 minutes. Remove the shrimp to a dish.

2. Reheat the oil and add the ginger and garlic, and fry for 1 minute.

3. Add the onions and stir-fry for 1 minute.

4. Add the leek, peas and bean sprouts. Fry for 2-3 minutes.

5. Sprinkle over the seasoning ingredients and return the shrimp to the wok. Cover and cook for 20 minutes. Serve immediately.

TIME: Preparation takes 10 minutes, cooking takes 10 minutes.

BUYING GUIDE: Always buy bean sprouts on the day your intend to use them, as they deteriorate rapidly.

SHRIMP IN HOT SAUCE

A quick dish that is perfect for a mid-week treat.

SERVES 2

12oz cooked unshelled shrimp

Seasoning
1 tsp malt vinegar
1 tsp Shao Hsing wine or dry sherry
Pinch salt

Sauce
1 tsp cornstarch mixed with 1 tbsp
    water
2 tsps tomato paste
Salt and freshly ground black pepper to
    taste
2 tsps sugar
½ tsp monosodium glutamate (optional)
1 tsp hot chili sauce
1 cup chicken stock

2 tbsps cooked oil
1 onion, chopped
1 stick celery, sliced
1 clove garlic, peeled and crushed

1. Wash shrimp and drain well. Mix the seasoning ingredients together.

2. Mix the sauce ingredients together in a separate bowl.

3. Heat the oil in a wok and deep-fry the shrimp for 1 minute. Remove the shrimp and drain. Keep the oil.

4. Reheat the wok and add 2 tsps oil and stir-fry the onion, celery and garlic for 1 minute.

5. Add shrimp and blended sauce ingredients. Bring to the boil and simmer gently for 3-4 minutes. Stir in the seasoning mixture.

TIME: Preparation takes 10 minutes, cooking takes 6 minutes.

SWEET-SOUR FISH

*In China this dish is almost always prepared with freshwater
fish, but sea bass is also an excellent choice.*

SERVES 2

1 sea bass, gray mullet or carp, weighing
   about 2lbs, cleaned
1 tbsp dry sherry
Few slices fresh ginger
½ cup sugar
7 tbsps cider vinegar
1 tbsp soy sauce
2 tbsps cornstarch
1 clove garlic, crushed
2 green onions, shredded
1 small carrot, peeled and finely shredded
½ cup bamboo shoots, shredded

1. Rinse the fish well inside and out. Make
three diagonal cuts on each side of the
fish with a sharp knife.

2. Trim off the fins, leaving the dorsal fin
on top.

3. Trim the tail to two neat points.

4. Bring enough water to cover the fish to
boil in a wok. Gently lower the fish into
the boiling water and add the sherry and
ginger. Cover the wok tightly and remove
at once from the heat. Allow to stand 15-
20 minutes to let the fish cook in the
residual heat.

5. To test if the fish is cooked, pull the
dorsal fin – if it comes off easily the fish is
done. If not, return the wok to the heat
and bring to the boil. Remove from the
heat and leave the fish to stand a further 5
minutes. Transfer the fish to a heated
serving dish and keep it warm.

6. Take all but 4 tbsps of the fish cooking
liquid from the wok. Add the remaining
ingredients including the vegetables and
cook, stirring constantly, until the sauce
thickens. Spoon some of the sauce over
the fish to serve and serve the rest
separately.

TIME: Preparation takes about 25 minutes, cooking takes about 15-25 minutes.

COOK'S TIP: The diagonal cuts in the side of the fish ensure even cooking.

VARIATION: If desired, use smaller fish such as trout or red mullet and shorten the cooking
time to 10-15 minutes.

PREPARATION: The fish may also be cooked in the oven in a large roasting pan or in
greased foil sprinkled with sherry. Cook at 375°F for 10 minutes per ½-inch thickness,
measured around the middle of the fish.

STEAMED SHRIMP

*Fresh shrimp, garnished with zucchini peel, steamed
and served with a fish-flavored sauce.*

SERVES 4

1 tbsp fish sauce
1 tbsp water
1 tbsp wine vinegar
1 tbsp soy sauce
2 tsps sugar
10 fresh mint leaves, finely chopped
1 shallot, chopped
Salt and pepper
12 fresh shrimp, peeled and cleaned
2 medium-sized zucchini, peeled and
　the peel cut into long strips

1. Mix together the fish sauce, water,
vinegar, soy sauce, sugar, mint, shallot
and salt and pepper. Stir well and set
aside for a least 1 hour.

2. Just before serving time, season the
shrimp with plenty of salt and pepper.

3. Roll the strips of zucchini peel around
the shrimp and cook them in a Chinese
steamer for 5 minutes.

4. Serve the shrimp piping hot,
accompanied with the sauce.

TIME: Preparation takes about 20 minutes and cooking takes about
10 minutes for 2 batches.

COOK'S TIP: If the strips of zucchini peel are not very pliable, blanch them in boiling
water for 3 seconds, before wrapping around the shrimp.

WATCHPOINT: The sauce can be prepared just before cooking the shrimp,
but it is much tastier if prepared at least 1 hour in advance.

SHRIMP WITH BROCCOLI

This dish is also suitable as an appetizer in small quantities.

SERVES 4

1lb peeled shrimp
Oil for deep frying

Sauce
1 cup chicken stock
2 tsps cornstarch
Freshly ground black pepper and salt to
taste
Pinch monosodium glutamate (optional)
1 tsp sugar

Seasoning
2 tbsps cooked oil, or oil from deep
frying the shrimp
Pinch salt
½ tsp sugar
Pinch monosodium glutamate (optional)
2 tsps cornstarch

8oz broccoli cut into 3-inch pieces
1 carrot, peeled and sliced
2 cloves garlic, peeled and chopped
½ inch fresh root ginger, peeled and
chopped

1. Deep-fry the shrimp in hot oil for 1-2 minutes. Drain the shrimp and keep to one side. Keep the oil.

2. Mix the sauce ingredients together. Mix the seasoning ingredients together in a separate bowl.

3. Cook the broccoli in boiling water for 1 minute. Drain and add cold water to cover. Drain once again and mix the broccoli with the seasoning ingredients.

4. Heat the wok and add 2 tbsps cooked oil. Add the carrot, garlic and ginger and stir-fry for 1 minute. Add the broccoli and stir-fry for 1 minute more.

5. Add the shrimp and stir-fry for ½ minute then add the blended sauce ingredients. Cook gently until the sauce thickens. Serve immediately.

TIME: Preparation takes 10 minutes, cooking takes 8-10 minutes.

SZECHUAN FISH STEAK

Szechuan food is hot and this recipe makes a wonderfully zippy fish dish.

SERVES 4

1½lbs haddock
2 tsps salt
2 tbsps cornstarch
1 egg

Sauce
1 large onion
2 cloves garlic
3 slices ginger root
2 chili peppers
2 slices Szechuan Ja Chai pickle (see
   Cook's Tip)
1 dried chili
Oil for deep frying
7 tbsps chicken stock
3 tbsps soy sauce
2 tbsps tomato paste
2 tbsps Hoisin sauce
1 tbsp sugar
1 tbsp wine vinegar
2 tbsps pale sherry

1. Cut fish into 2 x 1-inch oblong pieces. Rub with salt. Blend the cornstarch with the egg. Dip the fish in the egg mixture to coat on both sides.

2. Thinly slice the onion. Finely chop the garlic, ginger, chilies, pickle and dried chili.

3. Heat 4 tbsps oil in a large frying pan. Add the onion and other chopped vegetables and stir-fry for 2 minutes.

4. Add the stock, soy sauce, paste, Hoisin sauce, sugar, vinegar, and sherry. Stir over a high heat until well reduced.

5. Heat about 4 cups oil in a deep fryer. When hot, add the fish and fry for 2 minutes. Remove and drain.

6. Place them in the pan of sauce. Simmer in the sauce for 5 minutes before serving.

TIME: Preparation takes 10 minutes, cooking takes 10 minutes.

COOK'S TIP: If you cannot obtain the Ja Chai pickle, substitute your favorite hot pickle.

CRISPY FISH WITH CHILI

Choose your favorite white fish for this recipe.

SERVES 4

450g/1lb fish fillets, skinned, bones removed, and cut into 1-inch cubes

Batter
½ cup all-purpose flour
1 egg, separated
1 tbsp oil
6 tbsps milk
Salt
Oil for deep frying

Sauce
1 tsp grated root ginger
¼ tsp chili powder
2 tbsps tomato paste
2 tbsps tomato chutney
2 tbsps dark soy sauce
2 tbsps Chinese wine or dry sherry
2 tbsps water
1 tsp sugar
1 red chili, seeds removed, and sliced finely
1 clove garlic, crushed
Salt
Pepper

1. Sift the flour with a pinch of salt. Make a well in the center, and drop in the egg yolk and oil.

2. Mix to a smooth batter with the milk, gradually incorporating the flour. Beat well. Cover and set aside in a cool place for 30 minutes.

3. Whisk egg white until stiff, and fold into batter just before using.

4. Heat oil in wok. Dip fish pieces into batter and coat completely. When oil is hot, carefully lower fish pieces in until cooked through and golden brown – about 10 minutes. Remove with a slotted spoon.

5. Reheat oil and refry each fish piece for 2 minutes. Remove with a slotted spoon and drain on paper towels.

6. Carefully remove all but 1 tbsp of oil from the wok.

7. Heat oil, add chili, ginger, garlic, chili powder, tomato paste, tomato chutney, soy sauce, sugar, wine and water, and salt and pepper to taste.

8. Stir well over heat for 3 minutes. Increase heat and toss in fish pieces. Coat with sauce and, when heated through, serve immediately.

TIME: Preparation takes 40 minutes, cooking takes 30 minutes.

COOK'S TIP: Choose your favorite type of fish for this recipe.

SEAFOOD CHOW MEIN

*Chinese noodles cooked with mussels, clams and
vegetables and served in a rich ginger
and wine flavored sauce.*

SERVES 4

8oz Chinese noodles
½ green pepper, seeded
½ red pepper, seeded
1 tbsp oil
½ tsp chopped garlic
½ tsp chopped fresh ginger root
½ green onion, chopped
5oz uncooked mussels (shelled)
2oz uncooked clams (shelled)
1 tbsp Chinese wine
2 tbsps soy sauce
Salt and pepper

1. Cook the noodles in boiling, salted
water. Rinse them under cold water and
set aside to drain.

2. Cut the peppers into thin slices.

3. Heat the oil in a wok and stir-fry the
garlic, ginger, peppers and green onion
for 1 minute.

4. Stir in the mussels, clams, Chinese wine,
soy sauce and the cooked noodles.

5. Mix together well, using chopsticks.
Season with salt and pepper and serve
when cooked through completely.

TIME: Preparation takes about 15 minutes and cooking takes approximately 15 minutes.

VARIATION: Add other types of seafood to this dish.

WATCHPOINT: In Step 5 heat the noodles thoroughly, turning
them in the sauce, to coat evenly.

KUNG PAO SHRIMP WITH CASHEW NUTS

*It is said that Kung Pao invented this dish, but
to this day no one knows who he was!*

SERVES 6

½ tsp chopped fresh ginger
1 tsp chopped garlic
1½ tbsps cornstarch
¼ tsp baking soda
Salt and pepper
¼ tsp sugar
1lb uncooked shrimp
4 tbsps oil
1 small onion, cut into dice
1 large or 2 small zucchini, cut into
    ½-inch cubes
1 small red pepper, cut into ½-inch cubes
2oz cashew nuts

Sauce
1 cup chicken stock
1 tbsp cornstarch
2 tsps chili sauce
2 tsps bean paste (optional)
2 tsps sesame oil
1 tbsp dry sherry or rice wine

1. Mix together the ginger, garlic,
1½ tbsps cornstarch, baking soda, salt,
pepper and sugar.

2. If the shrimp are unpeeled, remove the peels and the dark vein running along the rounded side. If large, cut in half. Place in the dry ingredients and leave to stand for 20 minutes.

3. Heat the oil in a wok and when hot add the shrimp. Cook, stirring over high heat for about 20 seconds, or just until the shrimp change color. Transfer to a plate.

4. Add the onion to the same oil in the wok and cook for about 1 minute. Add the zucchini and red pepper and cook about 30 seconds.

5. Mix the sauce ingredients together and add to the wok. Cook, stirring constantly, until the sauce is slightly thickened. Add the shrimp and the cashew nuts and heat through completely.

TIME: Preparation takes about 20 minutes, cooking takes about 3 minutes.

VARIATION: If using cooked shrimp, add with the vegetables.
Vary amount of chili sauce to suit your taste.

SERVING IDEA: Serve with plain or fried rice.

Meat

Pork and Shrimp Chow Mein
Lamb with Tomatoes
Sweet and Sour Beef
Pork Spare Ribs
Beef with Broccoli
Fillet Steak Chinese Style
Pork with Green Peppers
Five-Spice Beef with Broccoli
Beef with Onions
Sweet and Sour Pork
Spiced Beef
Meat and Shrimp Chow Mein
Sweet and Sour Pork and Pineapple
Stir-fry Beef with Mango Slices
Caramelized Spareribs
Beef with Green Pepper and Chili
Beef Steak with Ginger
Pork Meat Balls in Sauce
Peking Beef
Lamb Curry
Sweet Pork with Vegetables
Braised Hong Kong Beef
Beef with Green Beans
Diced Pork with Walnuts
Beef with Tomato and Pepper
in Black Bean Sauce
Pork with Black Bean Sauce

PORK & SHRIMP CHOW MEIN

*Chinese chow mein dishes are usually based on noodles,
using more expensive ingredients in small amounts.
This makes economical everyday fare.*

SERVES 4-6

8oz medium dried Chinese noodles
Oil
8oz pork tenderloin, thinly sliced
1 carrot, peeled and shredded
1 small red pepper, cored, seeded and
    thinly sliced
2 cups bean sprouts
2oz snow peas
1 tbsp rice wine or dry sherry
2 tbsps soy sauce
1 cup peeled, cooked shrimp

1. Cook the noodles in plenty of boiling salted water for about 4-5 minutes. Rinse under hot water and drain thoroughly.

2. Heat the wok and add oil. Stir-fry the pork 4-5 minutes or until almost cooked. Add the carrots to the wok and cook for 1-2 minutes.

3. Add the red pepper and add the remaining vegetables, wine and soy sauce. Cook for about 2 minutes.

4. Add the cooked, drained noodles and shrimp and toss over heat for 1-2 minutes. Serve immediately.

TIME: Preparation takes about 20 minutes. The noodles take 4-5 minutes to cook and the stir-fried ingredients need to cook for about 5-6 minutes for the pork and about 3 minutes for the vegetables.

VARIATION: Use green pepper instead of red, or add other vegetables such as baby corn ears, mushrooms or peas.

BUYING GUIDE: Dried Chinese noodles are available in three thicknesses. Thin noodles are usually reserved for soup, while medium and thick noodles are used for fried dishes.

LAMB WITH TOMATOES

*Lamb and tomatoes make a wonderful,
if unusual, combination.*

SERVES 2

2 tsps cornstarch
½ tsp salt
1 tbsp light soy sauce
4 tbsps water
3 tbsps oil
½ inch fresh root ginger, sliced
½lb lamb fillet, cut across the grain in
    thin strips of ½ x 2 inches
2 green onions, chopped
1 onion, peeled and cut into 1-inch pieces
1 green pepper, seeded and cut into strips
1 tsp curry powder
3-4 small, firm tomatoes, cut into ½-inch
    pieces

1. Mix the cornstarch, salt, soy sauce, water and 1 tsp of the oil together. Put to one side.

2. Heat the remaining oil in a wok and fry the ginger and lamb for 2-3 minutes.

3. Add the onions, green pepper and curry powder and stir fry for 3-4 minutes.

4. Stir in the cornstarch mixture and cook for 1 minute.

5. Add the tomatoes and cook until the sauce thickens. Remove the slice of ginger before serving.

TIME: Preparation takes 20 minutes, cooking takes about 10 minutes.

BUYING GUIDE: Fresh root ginger is widely available.
When buying look for a plump, smooth root.

Sweet and Sour Beef

The combination of sweet and sour is an
old favorite for Chinese food lovers.

SERVES 2

Batter
1 cup all-purpose flour
1½ tsps baking powder
4 tbsps cornstarch
1 tbsp oil
3 tbsps oil
8oz fillet of beef, cut into 1-inch cubes
1 onion, peeled and cut into wedges
1 inch fresh root ginger, peeled and
    thinly sliced
1 clove garlic, peeled and crushed
1 green pepper, seeded and chopped

Sweet and Sour Sauce
4 tbsps sugar
¼ tsp salt
4 tbsps red or malt vinegar
1 tsp fresh root ginger, peeled and
    minced
6 tbsps water
1 tbsp cornstarch or arrowroot
2 tsps cooked oil
Few drops food coloring
Oil for deep frying

1. For the batter: sieve the flour, baking powder and cornstarch.

2. Beat in the 1 tbsp oil and add sufficient water to make a thick, smooth batter.

3. Heat the 3 tbsps oil in a wok and stir-fry the beef for 2 minutes. Remove the beef.

4. Fry the onion, ginger, garlic and green pepper for 2-3 minutes in the same oil. Remove the wok from the heat.

5. Mix the sauce ingredients together and add to the wok. Return the wok to the heat and bring to the boil gently. Lower the heat and simmer gently for 2-3 minutes until thick and clear.

6. Meanwhile, dip the beef cubes into the batter and deep fry in the hot oil until golden brown and crisp.

7. Drain on paper towels. Arrange in a deep dish and pour the hot sauce over the beef. Serve with a chow mein dish or fried rice.

TIME: Preparation takes 15 minutes, cooking takes 15 minutes.

VARIATION: Thinly sliced carrots, cucumber and zucchini may also be added along with the onion, ginger and green pepper.

PORK SPARERIBS

A great restaurant favorite which tastes just as good made at home.

SERVES 4

16-20 spareribs
1 tsp salt
Oil
1 tsp ginger paste
1 tsp garlic paste
1 tsp onion paste
Pinch monosodium glutamate (optional)
1 tsp light soy sauce
1 tsp cornstarch
1 egg
½ tsp Shao Hsing wine or dry sherry
½ tsp chili oil

Sauce
3 tbsps sugar
3 tbsps black vinegar
1 tbsp tomato catsup (optional)
1 tsp cornstarch
1 tsp water
1 tbsp dark soy sauce
½ tsp salt
½ tsp freshly ground black pepper

---

1. Trim excess fat from spareribs and rub with salt. Add 4 tbsps oil to the wok and fry the ginger, garlic and onion for 1-2 minutes. Add the spareribs and stir-fry for 6 minutes.

2. Remove to a dish and add the monosodium glutamate, light soy sauce, cornstarch, egg, wine and chili oil. Marinate for 10 minutes.

3. Prepare the sauce by mixing all the sauce ingredients together in the wok and bringing them gently to the boil. Simmer for 2-3 minutes and add the spareribs along with their marinade. Stir fry until the liquid is reduced to half its original quantity.

4. Put all the ingredients onto a roasting pan and spread out evenly. Bake at 375°F, for 25 minutes. Baste occasionally with the liquid from the tray and oil. The spareribs should have browned well and be well coated with seasoning. Serve hot or cold.

TIME: Preparation takes 25 minutes, cooking takes 40-45 minutes.

BUYING GUIDE: Monosodium glutamate is available in most supermarkets.

BEEF WITH BROCCOLI

*The traditional Chinese method of cutting meat for
stir-frying, used in this recipe, ensures that the
meat will be tender and will cook quickly.*

SERVES 2-3

1lb rump steak, partially frozen
4 tbsps dark soy sauce
1 tbsp cornstarch
1 tbp dry sherry
1 tsp sugar
8oz fresh broccoli
1-inch piece ginger, peeled and
    shredded
6 tbsps oil
Salt and pepper

1. Trim any fat from the meat and cut into
very thin strips across the grain. Strips
should be about 3-inches long.

2. Combine the meat with the soy sauce,
cornstarch, sherry and sugar. Stir well and
leave long enough for the meat to
completely defrost.

3. Trim the florets from the stalks of the
broccoli and cut them into even-sized
pieces. Peel the stalks of the broccoli and
cut into thin, diagonal slices.

4. Slice the ginger into shreds. Heat a wok
and add 2 tbsps of the oil to it. Add the
broccoli and sprinkle with salt and
pepper. Stir-fry, turning constantly, until
the broccoli is dark green. Do not cook
for longer than 2 minutes. Remove from
the wok and set aside.

5. Place the remaining oil in the wok and
add the ginger and beef. Stir-fry, turning
constantly, for about 2 minutes. Return the
broccoli to the pan and mix well. Heat
through for 30 seconds and serve
immediately.

TIME: Preparation takes about 25 minutes and cooking takes about 4 minutes.

PREPARATION: Using meat that is partially frozen makes it easier to get very thin slices.

COOK'S TIP: If more sauce is desired, double the quantities of
soy sauce, cornstarch, dry sherry and sugar.

FILLET STEAK CHINESE STYLE

Fillet steak is best for this quick-fry recipe.

SERVES 4

8oz fillet or rump steak, cut into 1-inch
    pieces
Pinch of baking soda
1 tbsp light soy sauce
1 tsp sesame oil
1 tsp Chinese wine, or 2 tsps dry sherry
2 tsps sugar
1 tsp cornstarch
Salt
Pepper
2 tbsps dark soy sauce
4 tbsps water
2 tbsps peanut oil
2 cloves garlic, crushed
2 green onions, sliced diagonally into
    ½-inch pieces
½ tsp crushed ginger
1 can straw mushrooms, drained
1 can baby corn, drained
1 tbsp oyster sauce

Garnish
Green onion flowers (cut green onions
into 2 inch lengths. Carefully cut into fine
shreds, keeping one end intact, and then
soak in ice cold water until curling)

1. Put steak in a bowl and sprinkle over baking soda.

2. Mix together light soy sauce, sesame oil, wine, half the sugar, half the cornstarch, and seasoning. Pour over the steak and leave for at least one hour, turning meat occasionally.

3. Meanwhile, make sauce by mixing 2 tbsps of dark soy sauce, remaining sugar and cornstarch, and water. Mix together and set aside.

4. Heat wok, add peanut oil and, when hot, fry steak for 4 minutes. Remove from wok and set aside.

5. Add garlic, green onions, ginger, mushrooms, baby corn, and finally steak.

6. Add oyster sauce and mix well. Add sauce mixture and bring to the boil. Cook for 3 minutes, stirring occasionally.

7. Serve hot with rice, garnished with green onion flowers.

TIME: Preparation takes 1 hour 15 minutes, cooking takes 20 minutes.

PORK WITH GREEN PEPPERS

*A quickly-prepared stir-fried pork dish with
green peppers and a Hoisin-based sauce.*

SERVES 4

1lb pork fillet
2 tbsps oil
½ tsp chopped garlic
2 green peppers, seeded and cut into thin
    matchsticks
1 tsp wine vinegar
2 tbsps chicken stock
1 tbsp Hoisin sauce
Salt and pepper
1 tsp cornstarch, combined with a little
    water

1. Slice the pork thinly, then cut into
narrow strips. Heat the oil in a wok. Add
the garlic, green pepper and the meat. Stir
together well. Cook for 1 minute, shaking
the wok occasionally.

2. Stir in the vinegar, stock and Hoisin
sauce. Season to taste with salt and
pepper. Cook for 3 minutes.

3. Stir in the cornstarch and cook, stirring
continuously, until the desired consistency
is reached.

TIME: Preparation takes about 10 minutes and cooking takes 5 minutes.

VARIATION: Replace the green pepper with a red one.

WATCHPOINT: It is not necessary to add sugar to this sauce, as the
Hoisin sauce is sweet enough.

FIVE-SPICE BEEF WITH BROCCOLI

A traditional recipe boosted by the addition of five-spice powder.

SERVES 2

8oz fillet or rump steak
1 clove garlic, crushed
½ tsp finely grated ginger
½ tsp five-spice powder
2 tbsps peanut oil
4oz broccoli florets
Bunch of chives, snipped into
   1-inch lengths
½ tsp salt
1 tbsp dark soy sauce
¾ cup hot water
2 tsps cornstarch, slaked in 1 tbsp cold
   water

1. Cut steak into thin slices, then into narrow strips. Mix together with garlic, ginger, and five-spice powder.

2. Heat wok, add 1 tbsp of oil, and stir-fry broccoli for 8 minutes.

3. Remove broccoli and add remaining oil.

4. Add meat, and stir-fry for 3 minutes.

5. Add broccoli, soy sauce, salt and water, and heat to simmering point.

6. Mix cornstarch with cold water, and pour into wok, stirring continuously until liquid thickens.

7. Toss in chives, stir, and serve immediately with boiled rice.

TIME: Preparation takes 15 minutes, cooking takes 15 minutes.

BEEF WITH ONIONS

*Marinated beef, sautéed with onions, garlic and
ginger and served in a smooth sauce.*

SERVES 4

1lb fillet steak

Marinade
1 tbsp oil
1 tsp sesame oil
1 tbsp Chinese wine

1 tbsp oil
1 piece fresh ginger root, peeled and
    roughly chopped
3 onions, finely sliced
1 garlic clove, chopped
1¼ cups beef stock
1 pinch of sugar
2 tbsps dark soy sauce
1 tsp cornstarch, combined with a little
    water
Salt and pepper

1. Cut the fillet into very thin slices.

2. Mix together the marinade ingredients
and stir in the meat. Leave to marinate for
30 minutes.

3. Heat 1 tbsp oil in a wok and sauté the
ginger, onions and garlic until lightly
browned.

4. Lift the meat out of the marinade with a
slotted spoon and discard the marinade.
Add the meat to the wok and sauté with
the vegetables.

5. Pour over the stock, sugar and soy
sauce. Cook for 4 minutes.

6. Thicken the sauce with the cornstarch,
stirring continuously until the desired
consistency is reached. Season with salt
and pepper and serve immediately.

TIME: Preparation takes about 15 minutes and cooking takes approximately 20 minutes.

SERVING IDEA: Serve this dish on a bed of boiled or steamed white rice.

CHECKPOINT: If you use a wok, watch the cooking process carefully, as the
ingredients cook very quickly.

115

SWEET AND SOUR PORK

This really needs no introduction because of its popularity.
The dish originated in Canton, but is reproduced
in most of the world's Chinese restaurants.

SERVES 2-4

1 cup all-purpose flour
4 tbsps cornstarch
1½ tsps baking powder
Pinch salt
1 tbsp oil
Water
8oz pork fillet, cut into ½-inch cubes

1 onion, sliced
1 green pepper, seeded, cored and sliced
1 small can pineapple chunks, juice
   reserved
Oil for frying

Sweet and Sour Sauce
2 tbsps cornstarch
½ cup light brown sugar
Pinch salt
½ cup cider vinegar or rice
   vinegar
1 clove garlic, crushed
1 tsp fresh ginger, grated
6 tbsps tomato catsup
6 tbsps reserved pineapple juice

1. To prepare the batter, sift the flour, cornstarch, baking powder and salt into a bowl. Make a well in the center and add the oil and enough water to make a thick, smooth batter. Using a wooden spoon, stir the ingredients in the well, gradually incorporating flour from the outside, and beat until smooth.

2. Heat enough oil in a wok to deep-fry the pork. Dip the pork cubes one at a time into the batter and drop into the hot oil. Fry 4-5 pieces of pork at a time and remove them with a draining spoon to paper towels. Continue until all the pork is fried.

3. Pour off most of the oil from the wok and add the sliced onion, pepper and pineapple. Cook over high heat for 1-2 minutes. Remove and set aside.

4. Mix all the sauce ingredients together and pour into the wok. Bring slowly to the boil, stirring continuously until thickened. Allow to simmer for about 1-2 minutes or until completely clear.

5. Add the vegetables, pineapple and pork cubes to the sauce and stir to coat completely. Reheat for 1-2 minutes and serve immediately.

TIME: Preparation takes about 15 minutes, cooking takes about 15 minutes.

VARIATION: Use beef or chicken instead of the pork. Uncooked, peeled shrimp may be used as can whitefish, cut into 1-inch pieces.

SPICED BEEF

A classic recipe which requires the best-quality beef.

SERVES 2-3

Marinade
1 tsp sugar
2-3 star anise, ground
½ tsp ground fennel
1 tbsp dark soy sauce
¼ tsp monosodium glutamate (optional)

1lb fillet of beef, cut into 1-inch strips
1 inch fresh root ginger, peeled and
   crushed
½ tsp salt
2 tbsps oil
4 green onions, sliced
½ tsp freshly ground black pepper
1 tbsp light soy sauce

1. Mix the marinade ingredients together.

2. Add the beef strips, ginger and salt, and marinate for 20 minutes.

3. Heat the oil in wok and stir-fry the onions for 1 minute.

4. Add the beef, ground pepper and soy sauce and stir-fry for 4-5 minutes.

TIME: Preparation takes 30 minutes, cooking takes 5-6 minutes.

COOK'S TIP: Fresh root ginger keeps well if wrapped in food wrap and stored in the refrigerator.

MEAT AND SHRIMP CHOW MEIN

*This chow mein is a wonderful mix
of vegetables, meat and seafood.*

SERVES 4

1lb dried Chinese noodles or broken
   spaghetti
¼ cup oil
2-3 green onions, chopped
4oz cooked ham, shredded
¾ cup peeled shrimp
4oz shredded carrots
4oz green beans, sliced
Salt to taste
1 tsp sugar
1 tbsp rice wine or dry sherry
4oz cooked chicken, shredded
2 cups bean sprouts
2½ tbsps soy sauce

1. Cook the noodles in boiling, salted water for 4-5 minutes. Rinse under cold water and drain thoroughly.

2. Toss in 1 tbsp oil. Heat the remaining oil in a wok.

3. Add the onions, ham, shrimp, carrots and green beans and stir-fry for 2-3 minutes.

4. Add the salt, sugar, wine, chicken and bean sprouts. Cook for 2 minutes.

5. Add the cooked noodles and soy sauce. Cook for 1-2 minutes. Serve immediately.

TIME: Preparation takes 20 minutes, cooking takes 12-15 minutes.

SWEET AND SOUR PORK AND PINEAPPLE

*Sweet and sour recipes are perfect for mixed
gatherings as children often enjoy them as much as adults.*

SERVES 4

1lb lean pork fillet, cut into
   1-inch cubes
2 tbsps light soy sauce
2 tbsps white wine vinegar
2 tbsps tomato paste
1 tbsp sugar
2 tbsps peanut oil
1 tbsp cornstarch
1 clove garlic, crushed
1 tsp grated root ginger
½ cup water
1 can pineapple pieces, drained
Fresh Chinese parsley (cilantro) to garnish

1. Place pork in bowl. Pour over light soy sauce and toss together. Leave for 15 minutes.

2. Mix together vinegar, tomato paste and sugar, and set aside.

3. Heat wok and add oil. Remove pork from soy sauce, and add soy sauce to sauce mixture.

4. Toss pork in cornstarch, coating well. When oil is hot, brown pork well all over.

5. Remove from pan and reduce heat. Fry garlic and ginger for 30 seconds.

6. Add water. Bring to the boil, then return pork to wok. Reduce heat, cover and simmer for 15 minutes, stirring occasionally.

7. Add sauce mixture and pineapple, and simmer for a further 15 minutes. Garnish with Chinese parsley.

TIME: Preparation takes 20 minutes, cooking takes 45 minutes.

SERVING IDEA: Serve with rice or noodles.

STIR-FRY BEEF WITH MANGO SLICES

This oriental combination of ingredients is refreshingly different.

SERVES 2-3

½lb fillet of beef
1 tbsp cooking wine
1 tbsp soy sauce
1 tsp cornstarch
¼ tsp sugar
¼ tsp pepper
1 large mango
4 tbsps oil
1 tbsp shredded ginger root
1 tbsp shredded green onions

1. Cut beef into thin bite-sized slices. Marinate in the wine, soy sauce, cornstarch, sugar and pepper for 20 minutes.

2. Skin mango, cut into ¼-inch thick slices.

3. Set wok over a high heat, pour 4 tbsps oil into the wok, wait until it's almost smoking. Reduce heat to moderate, stir-fry the beef and ginger for 1-2 minutes. Remove with a slotted spoon.

4. Toss the mango slices in the hot oil for a few seconds, return the beef and ginger, and green onions. Stir over the heat for a further few seconds. Serve immediately.

TIME: Preparation takes 30 minutes, cooking takes about 3 minutes.

COOK'S TIP: If you cannot get a fresh mango – canned mango is available from supermarkets.

CARAMELIZED SPARERIBS

These sweet, caramelized spareribs are always a success. Tell guests to use their fingers; knives or chopsticks are out of the question.

SERVES 4

1 carrot
1 bay leaf
1 leek
2lbs pork spareribs, separated
1 tbsp honey
1 tbsp white wine vinegar
1 tsp chopped garlic
2 tbsps soy sauce
⅓ cup chicken stock
Salt and pepper

1. In a large saucepan combine 4 cups water with the carrot, bay leaf and leek. Bring to the boil and add the spareribs. Blanch the meat for 10 minutes, remove from the stock and drain well.

2. Lay the ribs in an ovenproof pan. Combine the honey, vinegar and garlic, and spread the mixture on the ribs.

3. Add the soy sauce and the stock to the dish. Season well with salt and pepper.

4. Put into a very hot oven, 475°F, and cook until the ribs are caramelized and have turned a rich, dark brown color.

TIME: Preparation takes about 5 minutes and cooking takes approximately 55 minutes, from start to finish.

SERVING IDEA: Serve on a bed of finely shredded lettuce leaves, lightly seasoned with salt and pepper.

BEEF WITH GREEN PEPPER AND CHILI

*The classic mix of beef and green pepper is
given extra punch by the addition of chili peppers.*

SERVES 4

1lb fillet of beef, cut into 1-inch strips
Seasoning
2 tbsps dark soy sauce
1 tsp sesame oil
Pinch baking soda
¼ tsp ground black pepper
½ tsp salt

Oil for cooking
2 green peppers, seeded and thinly sliced
1 onion, peeled and sliced
2 green onions, chopped
1 inch fresh root ginger, peeled and sliced
2 garlic cloves, peeled and chopped
3 green chilies, sliced

Sauce
2 tbsps chicken stock
½ tsp monosodium glutamate (optional)
1 tsp dark soy sauce
Salt to taste
Few drops sesame oil

1. Marinate beef with the seasoning ingredients for 15 minutes.

2. Heat 2 tbsps oil and stir-fry green pepper and onions for 2 minutes. Remove to a plate.

3. Reheat wok, add 2-3 tbsps oil and fry ginger, garlic and green chilies for 1 minute.

4. Add beef and stir-fry for 4-5 minutes. Add sauce ingredients, mixed together, and the fried peppers and onions. Stir-fry for a further 2 minutes, remove ginger slice and serve.

TIME: Preparation takes 30 minutes, cooking takes 10-12 minutes.

BEEF STEAK WITH GINGER

Fresh root ginger accentuates the beef perfectly in this spicy recipe.

SERVES

Seasoning
½ tsp baking soda
3 tbsps light soy sauce
2 tbsps rice wine or dry sherry
½ tsp salt
½ tsp ground black pepper

½ tsp fresh root ginger, peeled and ground
½lb beef fillet, sliced into 1-inch pieces

Sauce
1 tsp sugar
¼ tsp monosodium glutamate (optional)
1 tbsp dark soy sauce
3 tbsps stock
Few drops sesame oil
1 tsp Shao Hsing wine or dry sherry

4 tbsps oil
1 inch fresh root ginger, peeled and
  thinly sliced
4 green onions, chopped
1 cup bamboo shoots, thinly sliced
2 green chilies, sliced

1. Mix the seasoning ingredients with the ground ginger. Add the beef and marinate for 20 minutes. Drain the beef and discard the marinade.

2. Mix the sauce ingredients together.

3. Heat 3 tbsps oil in the wok and fry the sliced ginger and onion for 2 minutes.

4. Add the bamboo shoots and chilies and stir-fry for 2 minutes. Remove to a plate.

5. Add the remaining oil to the wok and fry the beef for 2-3 minutes.

6. Add fried vegetables and stir-fry for 2 minutes. Add well-stirred sauce ingredients and simmer gently as the mixture thickens. Simmer another 1-2 minutes. Remove from heat and serve.

TIME: Preparation takes 20-25 minutes, cooking takes 10-12 minutes.

PORK MEAT BALLS IN SAUCE

This delicious dish is well worth the effort.

SERVES 4

Seasoning
Pinch monosodium glutamate (optional)
1 tbsp Shao Hsing wine or dry sherry
1-inch fresh root ginger, peeled and ground
2 green onions, white part only, minced
½ tsp salt
2 tsps cornstarch

1lb lean pork, ground
1oz bamboo shoots, chopped
2oz dried Chinese mushrooms, soaked,
    drained and sliced
1 egg, beaten
Cornstarch to roll the meatballs in
6oz Chinese white cabbage, cut into 3-inch
    pieces or 8oz ordinary green leafy
    cabbage, cut into 3-inch pieces
1 tbsp cooked oil
Oil for deep frying
1 tbsp cornstarch
3 tbsps water
1 small onion, peeled and finely chopped
1-inch fresh root ginger, peeled and
    finely chopped
1¼ cups chicken stock

Sauce
Salt to taste
½ tsp monosodium glutamate (optional)
1 tbsp light soy sauce
1 tsp dark soy sauce
1 tbsp cooked oil

1. Mix seasoning ingredients together.

2. Add the pork, bamboo shoots, mushrooms and egg and mix well.

3. Shape into 15-16 even-sized balls and roll them in cornstarch. Keep aside on a dish.

4. Blanch cabbage for 1 minute in boiling water and the cooked oil. Drain the cabbage and discard the water.

5. Heat the wok and add the oil for deep frying. When quite hot deep-fry the meat balls, a few at a time for 4-5 minutes. Remove and drain. Keep warm in a large cassrole dish.

6. Mix the cornstarch with the water and set aside.

7. Reheat the wok and add a teaspoon of oil. Stir-fry the ginger and onion for 2 minutes.

8. Add the chicken stock and stir in the blended sauce ingredients. Bring to the boil and add the meat balls. Simmer gently for 30 minutes.

9. Add the cabbage, sesame oil and the blended cornstarch mixture. Stir over the heat until sauce thickens.

TIME: Preparation takes 25 minutes, cooking takes 45 minutes.

BUYING GUIDE: Dried Chinese mushrooms are available in delicatessens and Chinese supermarkets.

PEKING BEEF

*In China, meat is often simmered in large earthenware
casseroles, but a wok is a convenient substitute.*

SERVES 8

2lb roast of beef
1¾ cups white wine
2½ cups water
2 whole green onions, roots trimmed
1-inch piece fresh ginger
3 star anise
2 tsps sugar
½ cup soy sauce
1 carrot, peeled
2 sticks celery
½ mooli (daikon) radish, peeled

1. Place the beef in a wok and add the white wine, water, green onions, ginger and anise. Cover and simmer for about 1 hour.

2. Add the sugar and soy sauce, stir and simmer for 30 minutes longer, or until the beef is tender. Allow to cool in the liquid.

3. Shred all the vegetables finely. Blanch them all, except the green onion, in boiling water for about 1 minute. Rinse under cold water, drain and leave to dry.

4. When the meat is cold, remove it from the liquid and cut into thin slices. Arrange on a serving plate and strain the liquid over it. Scatter over the shredded vegetables and serve cold.

TIME: Preparation takes about 25 minutes if shredding the vegetables by hand.
This can also be done with the fine shredding blade of a food processor.
Cooking takes about 1½ hours.

ECONOMY: Because of the long cooking time, less expensive cuts of meat may
be used for this dish.

COOK'S TIP: If using a rolled roast, remove as much of the fat from the outside as
possible. Skim off any fat that rises to the surface of the liquid as it cools, before
pouring over the meat to serve.

LAMB CURRY

*Lamb absorbs flavors well and is
therefore perfect for curries.*

SERVES 2-3

2 tbsps oil
1 onion, peeled and chopped
1 inch fresh root ginger, peeled and
    chopped
2 cloves of garlic, chopped
1lb lean, boned lamb, cut into cubes
1-2 carrots, scraped and sliced
1 tsp five-spice mixture
Salt to taste
2 chilies, chopped
1 tbsp tomato paste
2 tsps cornstarch
1 green pepper, seeded and chopped

1. Heat the oil and fry the onion for 2
minutes. Add the ginger and garlic and fry
for 1 minute.

2. Add the lamb and carrots and stir-fry for
3-4 minutes. Sprinkle over the five-spice
powder and add the salt, chilies and
tomato paste.

3. Stir in 1 cup water. Cover and simmer
for 30-35 minutes.

4. Mix 2 tbsps water with the cornstarch
and add to the curry.

5. Add the green pepper and simmer for 5
minutes. Serve with rice.

TIME: Preparation takes 15 minutes, cooking takes 50 minutes.

BUYING GUIDE: Five-spice is a mixture of some of the most commonly used spices in
Chinese cooking. It is available in supermarkets and delicatessens.

SWEET PORK WITH VEGETABLES

Pork with matchstick vegetables in a marvellous sweet sauce.

SERVES 4

1 onion
¼ cucumber
½ red pepper, seeded
½ green pepper, seeded
1 slice pineapple, fresh or canned
4 tbsps pineapple juice
3 tbsps wine vinegar
1 tsp chili sauce
1 tbsp sugar
½ tomato, peeled, seeded and crushed
1½ cups chicken stock
2 tbsps oil
1 tsp cornstarch, mixed with 1 tsp water
1lb pork, cut into thin strips
1 clove garlic, chopped
Salt and pepper

1. Cut the onion, cucumber, red and green pepper and pineapple into thin matchsticks.

2. In a small bowl, mix together the pineapple juice, vinegar, chili sauce, sugar, crushed tomato and chicken stock.

3. Heat the oil in a wok, stir-fry the pork and the garlic. Once the meat is golden brown, remove with a slotted spoon and set aside.

4. Add all the vegetables and the pineapple to the wok and stir-fry for 2 minutes.

5. Return the pork to the wok with the vegetables and pineapple and pour over the contents of the bowl. Cook for 3-4 minutes, stirring, and shaking the wok from time to time.

6. Thicken the sauce by adding the cornstarch gradually, stirring continuously until the desired consistency is reached. Season to taste with salt and pepper.

7. Serve piping hot.

TIME: Preparation takes about 25 minutes and cooking takes approximately 40 minutes.

VARIATION: Replace the pineapple juice with orange juice.

WATCHPOINT: The vegetables must be stir-fried quickly so that they remain slightly crisp.

BRAISED HONG KONG BEEF

*Cutting the meat into tiny strips reduces the
cooking time of this dish.*

SERVES 4

2 tbsps oil
1lb fillet of beef, sliced into
    matchstick-size strips
1 onion, peeled and sliced
1 inch fresh root ginger, peeled and cut
    into thin strips
3-4 fresh tomatoes, cut into thin wedges
½lb carrots, scraped and cut into 2-inch
    strips
2 tsps brown sugar
½ tsp five spice powder
2 tbsps light soy sauce
1 tbsp rice wine or dry sherry
2 tbsps water
Salt to taste

1. Heat the oil in a wok and fry the beef
for 3-4 minutes. Add the onion, ginger,
tomatoes and carrots. Stir fry for 2-3
minutes.

2. Add the sugar, five spice powder, soy
sauce, wine and water. Season with salt to
taste and cook gently for 8-10 minutes.

TIME: Preparation takes 30 minutes, cooking takes about 15-17 minutes.

BUYING GUIDE: If you cannot get five-spice powder from
the supermarket try a health food store.

BEEF WITH GREEN BEANS

A typically Chinese sauce brings this combination alive.

SERVES 2-3

Seasoning
½ tsp baking soda
1 tsp cornstarch
1 tbsp light soy sauce
2 tbsps water
1 tsp cooked oil
1lb lean beef, thinly sliced into 1-inch pieces

Sauce
¼ tsp salt
1 tsp monosodium glutamate (optional)
1 tsp light soy sauce
1 tsp dark soy sauce
1 tsp Shao Hsing wine or dry sherry
½ cup stock
2 tsps cornstarch
3 tbsps oil

2 cloves of garlic, peeled and sliced
1 onion, peeled and cut into wedges
1 inch fresh ginger root, peeled and
    sliced thinly
6oz Chinese long beans, cut into 3-inch
    pieces, or whole tender green beans
Salt and freshly ground black pepper to
    taste

1. Mix seasoning ingredients together. Add the beef and marinate for 20 minutes. Drain the meat and discard the marinade.

2. Mix the sauce ingredients together.

3. Heat 2 tbsps oil in the wok until it smokes. Reduce the heat add the garlic and the beef, and stir-fry for 3-4 minutes. Remove the meat and keep to one side.

4. Add the remaining oil to the wok and add the onion, ginger and long beans and stir-fry for 2-3 minutes. Add fried beef.

5. Cover and fry for a further minute. Stir in the sauce ingredients and bring to the boil. Simmer gently for 2-3 minutes.

6. Season with salt and pepper. Remove from heat and serve.

TIME: Preparation takes 30 minutes, cooking takes 12 minutes.

BUYING GUIDE: Monosodium glutamate should be available in supermarkets,
if not try a delicatessen.

DICED PORK WITH WALNUTS

Walnuts accentuate the pork perfectly in this tasty liaison.

SERVES 2

4oz shelled walnuts
Oil for deep-frying

Seasoning
1½ tsps light soy sauce
Few drops sesame oil
Salt and freshly ground black pepper to
    taste
1 tbsp oil
1 tbsp water
1 tbsp cornstarch
Pinch monosodium glutamate (optional)

½lb pork fillet, cut into cubes
1 carrot, thinly sliced
1 onion, peeled and cut into pieces
3 green onions, chopped
1 inch fresh root ginger, peeled and
    thinly sliced

Sauce
6 tbsps stock
1 tsp cornstarch

---

1. Cook the walnuts in boiling water for 3-4 minutes. Drain the nuts thoroughly.

2. Deep-fry the walnuts until lightly browned. Remove and drain. Use oil for cooking.

3 Mix the seasoning ingredients together and add the pork. Leave to marinate for 15 minutes. Discard marinade.

4. Heat 2 tbsps of the walnut oil in the wok and stir-fry the carrots for 2 minutes. Add the onions and root ginger and stir-fry for 1 minute.

5. Add 2 tsps of the sauce stock and remove to a plate. Add the drained pork cubes and 1 tbsp oil to the wok and stir fry for 4-5 minutes.

6. Mix the remaining stock and the cornstarch together for the sauce.

7. Return the walnuts and carrots to the wok, together with the blended sauce ingredients. Mix well and simmer until the sauce thickens.

8. Remove and serve immediately.

TIME: Preparation takes 30 minutes, cooking takes 16-18 minutes.

COOK'S TIP: Monosodium glutamate adds extra strength to the flavor of a dish.

Beef with Tomato and Pepper in Black Bean Sauce

*Black beans are a specialty of Cantonese cooking and give
a pungent, salty taste to stir-fried dishes.*

SERVES 6

2 large tomatoes
2 tbsps salted black beans
2 tbsps water
4 tbsps dark soy sauce
1 tbsp cornstarch
1 tbsp dry sherry
1 tsp sugar
1lb rump steak, cut into thin strips
1 small green pepper, seeded and cored
4 tbsps oil
¾ cup beef stock
Pinch pepper

1. Core tomatoes and cut them into 16 wedges. Crush the black beans, add the water and set aside.

2. Combine soy sauce, cornstarch, sherry, sugar and meat in a bowl and set aside.

3. Cut pepper into ½-inch diagonal pieces. Heat the wok and add the oil. When hot, stir-fry the green pepper pieces for about 1 minute and remove.

4. Add the meat and the soy sauce mixture to the wok and stir-fry for about 2 minutes. Add the soaked black beans and the stock. Bring to the boil and allow to thicken slightly. Return the peppers to the wok and add the tomatoes and pepper. Heat through for 1 minute and serve immediately.

TIME: Preparation takes about 25 minutes, cooking takes about 5 minutes.

SERVING IDEA: Serve with plain boiled rice.

WATCHPOINT: Do not add the tomatoes too early or stir the mixture too vigorously once they are added or they will fall apart.

VARIATION: Substitute snow peas for the green peppers in the recipe. Mushrooms may also be added and cooked with the pepper or snow peas.

PORK WITH BLACK BEAN SAUCE

A tasty recipe which brings together classic Chinese ingredients.

SERVES 2-3

8oz lean pork, cut into 1-inch cubes
1 tbsp oil
1 red pepper, cored, seeds removed, and
    sliced

Sauce
3 tbsps black soya beans, rinsed in cold
    water and crushed with back of a spoon
2 tbsps Chinese wine, or dry sherry
1 tsp grated ginger
2 tbsps light soy sauce
3 cloves garlic, crushed
1 tbsp cornstarch
½ cup water

---

1. Mix together black beans, wine, ginger, soy sauce and garlic.

2. Blend cornstarch with 2 tbsps of water and add to mixture.

3. Place pork in a bowl, and pour over sauce. Toss together well. Leave for at least 30 minutes.

4. Heat wok, add oil and stir-fry red pepper for 3 minutes. Remove and set aside.

5. Add pork, reserving marinade sauce. Stir-fry pork until browned well all over.

6. Add marinade sauce and remaining water. Bring to the boil. Reduce heat, cover, and gently simmer for about 30 minutes, until pork is tender, stirring occasionally. Add more water if necessary.

7. Just before serving, add red pepper and heat through. Serve with plain white rice.

TIME: Preparation takes 40 minutes, cooking takes 45 minutes.

BUYING GUIDE: Black soya beans are available from health food stores.

Poultry

Szechuan Chili Chicken

Deep-Fried Crispy Chicken

Chicken and Cashew Nuts

Peking Egg Battered Chicken with Bean
Sprouts, in Onion and Garlic Sauce

Roast Crispy Duck

Chicken with Cloud Ears

Chicken Chop Suey

Chicken Fry with Sauce

Chicken with Walnuts and Celery

Tangerine Peel Chicken

Chicken in Hot Pepper Sauce

Sliced Duck with Bamboo Shoots
and Broccoli

Steamed Chicken

Stewed Chicken and Pineapple

Soy Chicken Wings

Chicken with Bean Sprouts

Chicken and Mushrooms

Duck with Bamboo Shoots

Deep-Fried Chicken with Lemon Slices

SZECHUAN CHILI CHICKEN

If you like chilies this is sure to become a favorite.

SERVES 3-4

¾lb chicken breast meat, cooked
1 tsp salt
1 egg white
⅓ cup oil
1½ tbsps cornstarch
2 slices ginger root
2 small dried chili peppers
2 green or red peppers
2 fresh chili peppers
2 tbsps soy sauce
2 tbsps wine vinegar

1. Cut the chicken into bite-sized pieces. Add the salt, egg white, 1 tbsp oil, and cornstarch. Mix and rub these evenly over the chicken pieces to form a thin coating.

2. Chop the ginger, and dried chili. Cut the peppers into bite-sized pieces.

3. Heat the remaining oil in a wok. Add the ginger and chili peppers stir-fry for 1 minute.

4. Add the chicken pieces, separating them while stirring. Add the pepper, soy sauce and vinegar, and fry for a further 2 minutes.

5. Serve immediately with rice.

TIME: Preparation takes 5 minutes, cooking takes 5 minutes.

COOK'S TIP: Vary the amount of chili peppers according to how hot you like your food!

DEEP-FRIED CRISPY CHICKEN

Everybody loves fried chicken and this recipe is especially tasty.

SERVES 4

3-4lbs chicken, prepared for cooking

Seasoning
1 tsp salt
½ tsp five-spice powder
1½oz maltose
2 tbsps malt vinegar
1 cup white vinegar
Oil for deep frying

1. Wash the chicken and hang it up by a hook to drain and dry. The skin will dry quickly. Pour boiling water over the chicken 4-5 times, to partially cook the skin. This will make the skin crisp during frying. Rub salt and five-spice powder well inside the chicken cavity.

2. Dissolve the maltose and vinegars in a pan over a gentle heat. Pour over the chicken. Repeat several times, catching the maltose solution in a drip tray.

3. Leave the chicken to hang and dry for 1½-2 hours, until the skin is smooth and shiny.

4. Heat the oil for deep frying. Deep-fry the chicken for 10 minutes. Ladle hot oil carefully over the chicken continually, until the chicken is deep brown in color. (The skin puffs out slightly.)

5. Cook for a further 3-4 minutes and remove from the oil. Drain on paper towels. Cut into small pieces and serve with a dip.

TIME: Preparation takes 3 hours, cooking takes 13-14 minutes.

COOKS TIP: Maltose is similar to molasses and can be substituted by honey or syrup.

CHICKEN AND CASHEW NUTS

A popular combination that works extremely well.

SERVES 4

12oz chicken breast, sliced into 1-inch
 pieces
1 tbsp cornstarch

Seasoning
1 tsp salt
1 tsp sesame oil
1 tbsp light soy sauce
½ tsp sugar

Oil for deep frying
1 cup cashew nuts
2 green onions, chopped
1 small onion, peeled and cubed
1 inch fresh root ginger, peeled and sliced
2 cloves of garlic, sliced
3oz snow peas
2oz bamboo shoots, thinly sliced

Sauce
2 tsps cornstarch
1 tbsp Hoisin sauce
¾ cup chicken stock
Pinch monosodium glutamate (optional)

---

1. Roll the chicken pieces in cornstarch.
Discard the remaining cornstarch.

2. Mix the seasoning ingredients together
and pour over chicken. Leave to stand for
10 minutes.

3. Heat oil for deep frying and fry cashew
nuts until golden brown. Remove the nuts
and drain on paper towels.

4. Heat 2 tbsps oil in a wok and stir-fry
the onions, ginger and garlic for 2-3
minutes.

5. Add snow peas and bamboo shoots and
stir-fry for 3 minutes. Remove the fried
ingredients.

6. Add 1 tbsp oil to the wok and fry the
chicken for 3-4 minutes. Remove the
chicken.

7. Clean the wok and add a further 2 tsps
oil and return chicken, cashew nuts and
fried onions etc. to the wok.

8. Prepare the sauce by mixing the
cornstarch, Hoisin sauce, chicken stock
and monosodium glutamate together.

9. Pour over the chicken. Mix well and
cook until the sauce thickens and
becomes transparent.

TIME: Preparation takes 15 minutes, cooking takes 15 minutes.

VARIATION: A few chunks of pineapple will add extra zest to the dish.

PEKING EGG BATTERED CHICKEN WITH BEAN SPROUTS, IN ONION AND GARLIC SAUCE

This exciting mixture results in a simply delicious dish.

SERVES 3

3 breasts of chicken
Salt and pepper
2 eggs
2 cloves garlic
2 green onions
2 cups bean sprouts
4 tbsps oil
4 tbsps stock
Vinegar to taste

1. Cut each chicken breast into thin slices. Rub with salt and pepper.

2. Beat eggs lightly, and add the chicken slices to the eggs.

3. Crush garlic and cut green onions into 1-inch pieces.

4. Heat the oil in the wok. Add the chicken pieces one by one, reduce heat to low and sauté for 2-3 minutes.

5. Once the egg has set, sprinkle the chicken with garlic, green onion and bean sprouts.

6. Finally, add the stock and vinegar to taste. Simmer gently for about 4 minutes.

7. Remove the chicken, cut each piece into small regular pieces, serve on a heated platter. Pour the remaining sauce from the pan over the chicken.

TIME: Preparation takes 10 minutes, cooking takes about 10 minutes.

COOK'S TIP: Buy the bean sprouts on the day you intend to use them as they deteriorate rapidly.

ROAST CRISPY DUCK

This dish can be served as a main course for 4 or as an appetizer for 6.

SERVES 4-6

4½lbs duck or goose, prepared for cooking
4 tbsps maltose or corn syrup
1 cup water
12 green onions, cut into 2-inch lengths
½ tsp red food coloring
2 tbsps tomato paste

Duck Dip
½ cup sugar
4 tbsps sweet bean paste
2 tbsps sesame oil
½ cup water

1. Wash the duck and pat it dry on a clean cloth. Ease the finger between the skin and flesh of the duck, starting at the neck end and working the length of the bird. Put a stick or large skewer through the neck and the cavity of the duck to wedge it securely. This will make the duck easier to handle. Hold the duck over the sink and pour boiling water all over it. Pat the duck dry.

2. Melt half the maltose and dissolve in the water. Stand the duck on a rack over a deep tray. Slowly pour the maltose liquid over the duck. Pour the maltose liquid over the duck 3 or 4 times. Leave the duck in a cool place for 6-8 hours, or overnight, until the skin is dry.

3. Remove the skewer. Stand the duck on a rack in a roasting pan. Preheat the oven to 400°F and cook for 30 minutes. Turn over and cook the underside for a further 30 minutes.

4. Melt the remaining maltose with the tomato paste and add the food coloring. Spread over the duck and cook for a further 30 minutes. (The duck should have a crisp, redish-brown skin.)

5. Heat the wok and add the mixed ingredients for the duck dip. Cook for 3-4 minutes until the sugar has dissolved and the dip is smooth. Serve in individual cups.

6. Remove the duck skin in squares. Slice the duck flesh and serve with the skin on top.

TIME: Preparation takes 15-20 minutes, plus 6-8 hours to dry, cooking takes 1 hour 30 minutes.

CHICKEN WITH CLOUD EARS

*Cloud ears is the delightful name for an edible
tree fungus which is mushroom-like in taste and texture.*

SERVES 6

---

12 cloud ears, wood ears or other dried
   Chinese mushrooms, soaked in boiling
   water for 5 minutes
1lb chicken breasts, boned and thinly sliced
1 egg white
2 tsps cornstarch
2 tsps white wine
2 tsps sesame oil
1-inch piece fresh ginger, left whole
1 clove garlic
1¼ cups oil
1¼ cups chicken stock
1 tbsp cornstarch
3 tbsps light soy sauce
Pinch salt and pepper

---

1. Soak the mushrooms until they soften
and swell. Remove all the skin and bone
from the chicken and cut it into thin slices.
Mix the chicken with the egg white,
cornstarch, wine and sesame oil.

2. Heat the wok for a few minutes and
pour in the oil. Add the whole piece of
ginger and whole garlic clove to the oil
and cook for about 1 minute. Take them
out and reduce the heat.

3. Add about a quarter of the chicken at a
time and stir-fry for about 1 minute.
Remove and continue cooking until all the
chicken is fried. Remove all but about 2
tbsps of the oil from the wok.

4. Drain the mushrooms and squeeze
them to extract all the liquid, if using
mushrooms with stems, remove the stems
before slicing thinly. Cut cloud ears or
wood ears into smaller pieces. Add to the
wok and cook for about 1 minute. Add
the stock and allow it to come almost to
the oil. Mix together the cornstarch and
soy sauce and add a spoonful of the hot
stock.

5. Add the mixture to the wok, stirring
constantly, and bring to the boil. Allow to
boil 1-2 minutes or until thickened. The
sauce will clear when the cornstarch has
cooked sufficiently.

6. Return the chicken to the wok and add
salt and pepper. Stir thoroughly for about
1 minute and serve immediately.

TIME: Preparation takes about 25 minutes, cooking takes about 5 minutes.

PREPARATION: If desired, the chicken may be cut into 1-inch cubes. If slicing, cut across
the grain as this helps the chicken to cook more evenly.

BUYING GUIDE: Cloud ears or wood ears are a type of edible Chinese tree fungus. They
are both available from Chinese supermarkets and some delicatessens. Chinese mushrooms
are more readily available from Chinese supermarkets and some delicatessens.

CHICKEN CHOP SUEY

*Give up the Chinese restaurant and create your own
delicious version of this great favorite.*

SERVES 2-3

2 tbsps light soy sauce
1 tsp brown sugar
Salt to taste
1lb boned chicken, cut into 1-inch pieces
2 tbsps cooking oil
1 onion, cut into chunks
2 cups bean sprouts
2 tsps sesame oil
¼ tsp monosodium glutamate (optional)
1 tbsp cornstarch
1 cup chicken stock

1. Mix the soy sauce with the sugar and salt and add the chicken pieces. Allow to marinate for 5 minutes. Drain the chicken and reserve the marinade.

2. Heat the wok and add the oil. Fry the chicken for 2-3 minutes. Remove the chicken.

3. Fry the onions for 2-3 minutes and add the bean sprouts. Stir-fry for 4-5 minutes.

4. Return the chicken to the pan and add the sesame oil.

5. Dissolve the monosodium glutamate and the cornstarch in the stock and pour over the chicken mixture. Cook for 2-3 minutes, stirring, until the sauce thickens.

TIME: Preparation takes 30 minutes, cooking takes 15 minutes.

COOK'S TIP: Bean sprouts should always be bought on the day they are to be used as they deteriorate rapidly.

CHICKEN FRY WITH SAUCE

*This recipe is perfect for using the less
popular parts of chicken, such as thighs.*

SERVES 2

1 tbsp cooked oil
1 tsp sesame oil
1oz sesame seeds

Sauce
2 cloves of garlic, minced
2 green onions, finely chopped or minced
1 tsp Chinese black vinegar or brown
   malt vinegar
3 tbsps dark soy sauce
1 tsp light soy sauce
½ tsp monosodium glutamate (optional)
½ tsp salt
1½ tsps sugar

8 chicken thighs, or 1lb chicken, cut
   into small joints

1. Heat the wok and add the oils. Stir-fry the sesame seeds till they change color to golden brown. Remove onto a dish.

2. Mix sauce ingredients together and add the sesame seeds.

3. Wipe the wok and add the chicken. Add sufficient water to cover, and cook for 20 minutes until the chicken is tender.

4. De-bone the chicken and quickly cut meat into bite-size pieces.

5. Arrange the chicken on a plate and spoon the sauce over the top. Serve immediately.

TIME: Preparation takes 20 minutes, cooking takes about 24 minutes.

CHICKEN WITH WALNUTS AND CELERY

Oyster sauce lends a subtle, slightly salty taste to this Cantonese dish.

SERVES 4

8oz boned chicken, cut into 1-inch pieces
2 tsps soy sauce
2 tsps brandy
1 tsp cornstarch
Salt and pepper
2 tbsps oil
1 clove garlic, peeled and crushed
1 cup walnut halves
3 sticks celery, cut in diagonal slices
¾ cup water or chicken stock
2 tsps oyster sauce

1. Combine the chicken with the soy sauce, brandy, cornstarch, salt and pepper.

2. Heat a wok and add the oil and garlic. Cook for about 1 minute to flavor the oil.

3. Remove the garlic and add the chicken in two batches. Stir-fry quickly without allowing the chicken to brown. Remove the chicken and add the walnuts to the wok. Cook for about 2 minutes until the walnuts are slightly brown and crisp.

4. Slice the celery, add to the wok and cook for about 1 minute. Add the oyster sauce and water and bring to the boil. When boiling, return the chicken to the pan and stir to coat all the ingredients well. Serve immediately.

TIME: Preparation takes 5 minutes, cooking takes about 15 minutes.

TANGERINE PEEL CHICKEN

*An exotic mixture of flavors blend perfectly
in this delicious chicken dish.*

SERVES 2

1lb boned chicken breast, cut into 1-inch
  pieces

Seasoning
½ tsp salt
1½ tsps sugar
½ tsp monosodium glutamate (optional)
1 tsp dark soy sauce
2 tsps light soy sauce
1 tsp rice wine or dry sherry
2 tsps malt vinegar
1 tsp sesame oil
2 tsps cornstarch

Oil for deep frying
1-2 red or green chilies, chopped
½ inch fresh root ginger, peeled and
  finely chopped
2 inches dried tangerine peel, coarsely
  ground or crumbled
2 green onions, finely chopped

Sauce
½ tsp cornstarch
1-2 tbsps water or stock

1. Mix the chicken pieces with the seasoning ingredients and stir well. Leave to marinate for 10-15 minutes. Remove the chicken pieces and reserve the marinade.

2. Heat wok and add the oil for deep frying. Once it starts to smoke add the chicken pieces and fry for 4-5 minutes until golden. Drain chicken on paper towels.

3. Pour off the oil, leaving 1 tbsp oil in the wok, and stir-fry the chilies, ginger, tangerine peel and onions for 2-3 minutes. When they begin to color add the chicken and stir-fry for 1 minute.

4. Mix the reserved marinade with the sauce ingredients and pour over the chicken. Stir and cook for 2-3 minutes until the sauce thickens and the chicken is tender. Serve immediately.

TIME: Preparation takes 30 minutes, cooking takes 12-15 minutes.

CHICKEN IN HOT PEPPER SAUCE

Stir-fried chicken served with peppers in a hot sauce.

SERVES 4

1 chicken
2 tbsps oil
1 tsp chopped garlic
1 green pepper, seeded and cut into thin
 strips
1 red pepper, seeded and cut into thin
 strips
1 tsp wine vinegar
1 tbsp light soy sauce
1 tsp sugar
1⅓ cups chicken stock
1 tbsp chili sauce
Salt and pepper

1. First, bone the chicken. To bone the legs, cut down along the bone on all sides, drawing out the bone with an even movement. Cut all the chicken meat into thin strips.

2. Heat the oil in a wok and stir-fry the garlic, chicken and the green and red peppers.

3. Pour off any excess oil and deglaze the wok with the vinegar. Stir in the soy sauce, sugar and stock.

4. Gradually stir in the chili sauce, tasting after each addition. Season with a little salt and pepper to taste.

5. Cook until the sauce has reduced slightly. Serve piping hot.

TIME: Preparation takes 10 minutes and cooking takes approximately 25 minutes.

SLICED DUCK WITH BAMBOO SHOOTS AND BROCCOLI

*A delightful recipe which mixes some of
China's best-loved ingredients.*

SERVES 2

2¼lb small duck
1 tsp monosodium glutamate (optional)
2½ tsps cornstarch
2 tbsps water
4oz broccoli, chopped
3 tbsps oil
2-3 green onions, chopped
1 inch fresh root ginger, peeled and
    thinly sliced
1 clove garlic, peeled and finely chopped
4oz bamboo shoots, sliced
½ tsp sugar
Salt and freshly ground black pepper to
    taste
¼ cup chicken stock
2 tsps rice wine or sweet sherry
Few drops sesame oil

1. Cut the duck flesh into bite-size pieces,
removing all the bones.

2. Mix the the monosodium glutamate,
1½ tsps cornstarch and 1 tbsp water
together. Stir into the duck. Marinate for
20 minutes.

3. Cook the broccoli in boiling water for 1
minute. Drain thoroughly.

4. Heat the wok and add the oil. Stir-fry
the onions, ginger, garlic and bamboo
shoots for 1-2 minutes.

5. Add the duck pieces and stir-fry for 2-3
minutes. Add the sugar, salt and pepper to
taste, stock, rice wine, sesame oil and
broccoli. Stir-fry for 3 minutes.

6. Add the remaining cornstarch and water
blended together. Stir over the heat until
the sauce thickens. Serve immediately.

COOK'S TIP: Fresh root ginger keeps well if tightly wrapped in
plastic wrap and stored in the refrigerator.

STEAMED CHICKEN

*A great method of cooking chicken and
one which brings out all its flavor.*

SERVES 3-4

1½lbs boned chicken

Seasoning
1 tbsp light soy sauce
1 tsp brown sugar
1 tsp salt
1 tbsp cornstarch
2 tbsps oil or cooked oil
½ tsp monosodium glutamate (optional)

4oz dried mushrooms, soaked in boiling
    water for 5 minutes and sliced, or
    ordinary mushrooms
½ inch fresh root ginger, peeled and
    sliced
4 green onions, finely chopped
2 tbsps stock or water, if needed

1. Cut the chicken into 1-inch pieces. Mix the seasoning ingredients together and mix with the chicken. Leave to marinate for 15 minutes.

2. Place a plate in a steamer and put the chicken, mushrooms, ginger, half the onion and the stock on top. Steam over boiling water for 15-20 minutes.

3. Serve with the remaining onions sprinkled over the chicken. The steaming can also be done on a greased lotus leaf or a banana leaf. The flavor is quite stunning.

TIME: Preparation takes 20-30 minutes, cooking takes 15-20 minutes.

COOK'S TIP: If you can obtain dried mushrooms do use them as their flavor is far superior to ordinary mushrooms.

STEWED CHICKEN AND PINEAPPLE

Pineapple complements the chicken wonderfully in this dish.

SERVES 2-3

Seasoning
2 tbsps light soy sauce
1 tbsp oil
1 tbsp cornstarch
1 tsp salt
½ tsp sesame oil
2 tbsps water

1½lbs boned chicken breast, cut into cubes

Sauce
1½ tsps cornstarch
1 cup water or chicken stock
2 tsps dark soy sauce
Salt to taste

2 tbsps oil
1 onion, peeled and cut into chunks
2 green onions, finely chopped
1 inch fresh root ginger, peeled and
   thinly sliced
4-5 pineapple rings, cut into chunks

1. Mix the seasoning ingredients together.

2. Add the cubed chicken and marinate for 10-12 minutes.

3. Mix the sauce ingredients together in a bowl.

4. Heat the oil in a wok and fry the onions for 2 minutes until just tender. Add the drained chicken and fry for 3-4 minutes.

5. Add the root ginger and fry for 1 minute.

6. Add any remaining marinade and the sauce ingredients and bring to the boil. Cook, stirring, until the sauce thickens then add the pineapple chunks. Heat through. Remove from the heat and serve with fried rice.

TIME: Preparation takes 30 minutes, cooking takes 15 minutes.

Soy Chicken Wings

These delicious chicken wings can be served on any occasion.

SERVES 4

2lbs chicken wings
½ tsp crushed root ginger
1 tbsp light soy sauce
1 tbsp sugar
1 tsp cornstarch
2 tsps sesame oil
1 tbsp Chinese wine, or
   2 tbsps dry sherry
Salt
Pepper
2 tbsps peanut oil
2 green onions, sliced
1 tbsp dark soy sauce
1 star anise
3 tbsps water

1. Wash chicken wings and dry on paper towels.

2. Mix together ginger, light soy sauce, sugar, cornstarch, sesame oil, wine, and seasoning. Pour marinade over chicken wings and leave for at least 1 hour, turning occasionally.

3. Heat peanut oil until very hot. Add green onions and chicken wings, and fry until chicken is browned well on all sides.

4. Add dark soy sauce, star anise and water. Bring to the boil, and simmer for 15 minutes.

5. Remove star anise. Serve hot or cold.

TIME: Preparation takes 1 hour 10 minutes, cooking takes 20 minutes.

CHICKEN WITH BEAN SPROUTS

*Marinated chicken, stir-fried with bean sprouts
and served with a sauce based on the marinade.*

SERVES 4

---

1 chicken, boned
1 tbsp Chinese wine
1 tsp cornstarch
2 cups bean sprouts
2 tbsps oil
½ green onion, finely sliced
1 tsp sugar
1¼ cups chicken stock
Salt and pepper

---

1. Bone the chicken and cut the meat into thin slices or strips.

2. Place the chicken on a plate and pour over the Chinese wine.

3. Sprinkle over the cornstarch and stir together well. Leave to marinate for 30 minutes.

4. Blanch the bean sprouts in boiling, lightly salted water for 1 minute. Rinse under cold running water and set aside to drain.

5. Remove the chicken from the marinade with a spoon. Heat the oil in a wok and stir-fry the onions and the chicken.

6. Add the drained bean sprouts and the sugar. Stir in the marinade and the stock. Allow the chicken to cook through, which will take approximately 20 minutes. Check the seasoning, adding salt and pepper to taste. Serve immediately.

TIME: Preparation takes about 20 minutes, marinating takes 30 minutes and cooking takes approximately 30 minutes.

VARIATION: Use an ordinary onion if green onions are not available.

WATCHPOINT: As soon as you add the marinade to the wok, the mixture will thicken so have the stock ready to pour in immediately and stir continuously until all the ingredients have been fully incorporated.

CHICKEN AND MUSHROOMS

A classic combination which always tastes great.

SERVES 2

Seasoning
½ tsp salt
2 tbsps light soy sauce
2 tsps cornstarch
1 tsp rice wine or dry sherry
Pinch monosodium glutamate (optional)

½lb chicken breast, cut into bite-size pieces

Sauce
Salt to taste
Freshly ground black pepper to taste
1 tbsp light soy sauce
1 cup chicken stock
2 tsps cornstarch or arrowroot
1 tsp oyster sauce

2 tbsps oil
1 onion, peeled and chopped
1 clove of garlic, sliced
½ inch fresh root ginger, peeled and
  thinly sliced
3 dried black mushrooms, soaked and
  sliced
2oz open mushrooms, sliced
2oz button mushrooms, sliced

1. Mix the seasoning ingredients together. Marinate the chicken in the seasoning mixture for 10 minutes.

2. Mix the sauce ingredients together.

3. Heat the oil in a wok and fry the onion, garlic and ginger for 2-3 minutes. Remove and put to one side.

4. Fry the drained chicken in the remaining oil for 4 minutes.

5. Add the mushrooms and stir-fry for 1 minute. Add a little extra oil if necessary.

6. Return the fried onion mixture to the wok and stir-fry until well mixed. Pour the blended sauce ingredients into the wok and cook gently until the sauce thickens. Serve piping hot.

TIME: Preparation takes 15 minutes, plus 10 minutes to marinate. Cooking takes 10-12 minutes.

COOK'S TIP: Supermarkets now have a wider range of mushrooms so choose your favorites if you cannot get those in the recipe.

Duck with Bamboo Shoots

Stir-fried bamboo shoots, served with duck breasts and Hoisin-based sauce.

SERVES 4

4oz bamboo shoots, cut into thin slices
¼ cup sugar
⅓ cup water
1 tsp chopped fresh ginger root
1 tbsp Hoisin sauce
2 duck breasts
1 tbsp oil
Salt and pepper

1. Cook the bamboo shoots in boiling, lightly salted water for approximately 15 minutes. Drain thoroughly and set aside.

2. Mix the sugar and water together in a small saucepan, stirring thoroughly.

3. Add the ginger and the Hoisin sauce. Place over a gentle heat and cook until a light syrup is formed.

4. Brush this syrup over the duck breasts.

5. Heat the oil in a frying pan and add the duck breasts, skin-side down first. Sear on each side. Take out and finish cooking in a hot oven, 425°F, for approximately 15 minutes.

6. Shortly before the duck breasts are cooked, stir-fry the bamboo shoots in the oil used to sear the duck breasts. Season with salt and pepper and serve hot with the sliced duck breasts.

TIME: Preparation takes about 10 minutes and total cooking time is approximately 50 minutes.

SERVING IDEA: Serve any leftover sauce in a small bowl to accompany the duck.

WATCHPOINT: Don't forget to begin searing the meat in the frying pan skin-side down and then finish with the other side.

DEEP-FRIED CHICKEN WITH LEMON SLICES

Lemon complements chicken perfectly in this quick dish.

SERVES 6-8

3lbs chicken breast meat
a) ½ tsp salt
   ½ tbsp cooking oil
   ½ tbsp light soy sauce
   1 tbsp cornstarch
   1 tbsp water
   1 egg yolk
   Black pepper
b) 6 tbsps cornstarch
   3 tbsps all-purpose flour
c) 3 tbsps sugar
   3 tbsps lemon juice
   6 tbsps light broth
   ½ tsp salt
   2 tbsps cornstarch
   1 tsp sesame oil
1 green pepper, cored and seeded
1 red pepper, cored and seeded
Oil for deep frying
2 lemons, thinly sliced
Chopped parsley

1. Skin the chicken. Cut into bite-sized, thin slices. Marinate chicken in a) for 10 minutes.

2. Mix b) on a plate and coat each chicken piece with the mixture.

3. Mix c) in a small bowl. Cut pepper into 1-inch pieces.

4. Place a 12-inch wok over a high heat. Heat the oil until almost smoking. Deep fry the chicken slices until golden brown.

5. Remove with a slotted spoon to a heated plate. Pour off all but a tablespoon of oil.

6. Stir-fry the pepper until it begins to brown. Pour in c). Bring to the boil, stirring until thickened.

7. Add the chicken pieces. Stir for a further few minutes. Transfer to a heated serving platter, and garnish with lemon slices and chopped parsley.

TIME: Preparation takes 20 minutes, cooking takes about 15 minutes.

Side Dishes

Bamboo Shoots with Green Vegetables
Stir-fried Rice with Peppers
Fried Vegetables with Ginger
Plain Fried Rice
Szechuan Eggplant
Fried Rice
Vegetable Stir-fry
Special Mixed Vegetables
Sweet and Sour Cabbage
Eggplant and Peppers Szechuan Style
Stir-Fried Sticky Rice

BAMBOO SHOOTS WITH GREEN VEGETABLES

This side dish is perfect with Peking duck.

SERVES 2

Oil for cooking
8oz chopped spinach, or chopped
   broccoli

Seasoning
½ cup chicken stock or water
¼ tsp monosodium glutamate (optional)
¼ tsp salt
¼ tsp sugar
4oz bamboo shoots, sliced

Sauce
1 tsp light soy sauce
Pinch monosodium glutamate
1 tsp cornstarch
2 tsps water
1 tbsp cooked oil

1. Heat 2 tbsps oil in the wok.

2. Fry the spinach for 2 minutes and add the mixed seasoning ingredients, except the bamboo shoots. Simmer for 1 minute and remove from the wok onto a dish.

3. Heat the wok and add 1 tbsp oil. Add the bamboo shoots and fry for 1-2 minutes.

4. Return the spinach mixture to the wok. Cook for 30 minutes.

5. Mix together the ingredients for the sauce. Add to the wok and cook for 1-2 minutes.

TIME: Preparation takes 10 minutes, cooking takes 10-12 minutes.

COOK'S TIP: Bamboo shoots should always be bought on the day they are to be used as they deteriorate rapidly.

STIR-FRIED RICE WITH PEPPERS

*Long grain rice stir-fried with red and
green peppers, onions and soy sauce.*

SERVES 4

6oz long grain rice
1 tbsp peanut oil
1 onion, chopped
1 green pepper, seeded and cut into small
    pieces
1 red pepper, seeded and cut into small
    pieces
1 tbsp soy sauce
Salt and pepper
1 tsp sesame oil

1. Cook the rice in boiling water, drain
and set aside.

2. Heat the oil in a wok and stir-fry the
onion, add the peppers and fry until
lightly browned.

3. Add the rice to the wok, stir in the soy
sauce and continue cooking until the rice
is heated through completely.

4. Season with salt, pepper and the
sesame oil, and serve.

TIME: Preparation takes 5 minutes and cooking takes approximately 25 minutes.

VARIATION: If you like the strong flavor of sesame oil, stir-fry the
vegetables and rice in this instead of the peanut oil.

WATCHPOINT: Do not overcook the rice in Step 1, or it will become sticky in Step 3.

FRIED VEGETABLES WITH GINGER

*Use your imagination with this recipe and adapt it
to whatever greens you can buy.*

SERVES 4-6

2¼lbs mixed Chinese green vegetables
   (cabbage, spinach, kale, broccoli,
   Chinese leaf etc.)
2oz snow peas
1 tsp baking soda
2 tsps sugar
1 tsp salt
2 tbsps oil
1 inch fresh root ginger, peeled and
   shredded
1 green pepper, seeded and diced
1 green or red chili, sliced into strips

Sauce
2 tsps dark soy sauce
1 tsp sugar
1 cup chicken stock
2 tsps cornstarch
1 tsp five spice powder

To Serve
½ tsp sesame oil
Freshly ground black pepper to taste

1. Cut greens into 3-inch pieces. Bring a large pan of water to the boil and add the sugar and salt.

2. Add the snow peas and greens and cook for 4-5 minutes. Drain green vegetables and discard water.

3. Add 1 tbsp oil to the vegetables and keep covered. Heat the remaining oil in the wok and stir fry the ginger for 1 minute.

4. Add the green pepper and chilies and stir-fry for 10-12 minutes. Add the blended sauce ingredients and stir well. Simmer gently for 3-4 minutes.

5. Add the green vegetables and cook for 1 minute. Serve immediately, sprinkled with sesame oil and pepper.

TIME: Preparation takes 10 minutes, cooking takes 13-15 minutes.

PLAIN FRIED RICE

*Producing perfect rice is a must
for lovers of Chinese food.*

SERVES

1lb long grain rice
¼ tsp monosodium glutamate
2 tbsps oil
Salt

1. Wash the rice in 4-5 changes of cold water. Drain the rice and put into a large pan or wok. Add sufficient cold water to come 1-inch above the level of the rice. Bring to the boil.

2. Stir once and reduce the heat to simmer. Cover and cook gently for 5-7 minutes until the water has been totally absorbed and the rice is separate and fluffy, with the necessary amount of stickiness to be handled by chopsticks.

3. Spread the rice out on a tray to cool. Sprinkle with the monosodium glutamate. Heat the oil in wok or large frying pan and add the rice. Stir fry for 1-2 minutes.

4. Add salt to taste and stir-fry for a further 1-2 minutes.

TIME: Preparation takes 5 minutes, plus cooling time, cooking takes 10-11 minutes.

SZECHUAN EGGPLANT

An unusual side-dish which adds extra spice to meals.

SERVES 2

Oil
1 large eggplant cut into 2-inch long and
    ½-inch thick strips
3 cloves garlic, peeled and finely sliced
1 inch fresh root ginger, peeled and
    shredded
1 onion, peeled and finely chopped
2 green onions, chopped
4oz cooked and shredded chicken
1 red or green chili, cut into strips

Seasoning
½ cup chicken stock
1 tsp sugar
1 tsp red vinegar or wine vinegar
½ tsp salt
½ tsp freshly ground black pepper

Sauce
1 tsp cornstarch
1 tbsp water
1 tsp sesame oil

1. Heat the wok and add 3 tbsps oil. Add eggplant and stir-fry for 4-5 minutes. The eggplant will absorb a lot of oil; keep stirring or else they will burn. Remove from wok and put to one side.

2. Heat the wok and add 2 tbsps oil. Add the garlic and ginger and fry for 1 minute.

3. Add the onions and fry for 2 minutes. Add the chicken and chili. Cook for 1 minute.

4. Return the eggplants to the wok. Add the blended seasoning ingredients and simmer for 6-7 minutes.

5. Stir in the blended sauce ingredients and simmer until the sauce thickens. Serve with extra sesame oil if desired.

TIME: Preparation takes 15 minutes, cooking takes 18-20 minutes.

COOK'S TIP: Vary the spiciness of this dish by increasing the quantity of chilies.

FRIED RICE

*A basic recipe for a traditional Chinese accompaniment to
stir-fried dishes, this can be more substantial with the
addition of meat, poultry or seafood.*

SERVES 6-8

1lb cooked rice, well drained and dried
3 tbsps oil
1 egg, beaten
1 tbsp soy sauce
½ cup cooked peas
Dash sesame oil
Salt and pepper
2 green onions, thinly sliced

1. Heat a wok and add the oil. Pour in the egg and soy sauce and cook until just beginning to set.

2. Add the rice and peas and stir to coat with the egg mixture. Allow to cook for about 3 minutes, stirring continuously. Add seasoning and sesame oil.

3. Spoon into a serving dish and sprinkle over the green onions.

TIME: The rice will take about 10 minutes to cook. Allow at least 20 minutes for it to drain as dry as possible. The fried rice dish will take about 4 minutes to cook.

VARIATION: Cooked meat, poultry or seafood may be added to the rice along with the peas.

COOK'S TIP: The 1lb rice measurement is the cooked weight.

VEGETABLE STIR-FRY

A marvellous blend of Chinese vegetables and nuts,
stir-fried in a little oil and then cooked in an aromatic sauce.

SERVES 4

2 dried lotus roots, soaked overnight in
  water
2 tbsps oil
1½ cups bean sprouts
½ red pepper, seeded and finely chopped
½ green pepper, seeded and finely
  chopped
½ green onion, chopped
1 head Chinese cabbage, finely chopped
3oz dried Chinese black mushrooms,
  soaked for 1 hour in warm water
1 zucchini thinly sliced
¾ cup frozen peas
2 tbsps cashew nuts, roughly chopped
1 tsp sugar
2 tbsps soy sauce
1¾ cups chicken stock
Salt and pepper

1. Cook the lotus roots in boiling, lightly salted water for 20 minutes. Slice thinly.

2. Heat the oil in a wok and stir-fry, in the following order, the bean sprouts, peppers, onion, Chinese cabbage, lotus root, mushrooms, zucchini, peas and cashew nuts.

3. Stir in the sugar, soy sauce and stock.

4. Season with salt and pepper and cook for 30 minutes, stirring frequently.

5. Serve the vegetables slightly drained of the sauce.

TIME: Preparation takes about 10 minutes and cooking takes approximately 35 minutes.

VARIATION: Any type of nut could be used in this recipe, for example walnuts, hazelnuts or almonds.

COOK'S TIP: If time permits, this recipe is even more delicious if the vegetables are stir-fried separately, each cooked vegetable being removed from the wok before continuing with the next. Finish by cooking all the vegetables together for 30 minutes in the chicken stock as above.

SPECIAL MIXED VEGETABLES

This dish illustrates the basic stir-frying technique for vegetables.

SERVES 4

1 tbsp oil
1 clove garlic, crushed
1-inch piece fresh ginger, sliced
4 Chinese cabbage leaves, shredded
2oz flat mushrooms, thinly sliced
2oz bamboo shoots, sliced
3 sticks celery, diagonally sliced
2oz baby corn, cut in half if large
1 small red pepper, cored, seeded and
    thinly sliced
1 cup bean sprouts
Salt and pepper
2 tbsps light soy sauce
Dash sesame oil
3 tomatoes, peeled, seeded and quartered

1. Heat the oil in a wok and add the ingredients in the order given, reserving the soy sauce, sesame oil and tomatoes.

2. To make it easier to peel the tomatoes, remove the stems and place in boiling water for 5 seconds.

3. Remove from the boiling water with a draining spoon and place in a bowl of cold water. This will make the peels easier to remove. Cut out the core end using a small sharp knife.

4. Cut the tomatoes in half and then in quarters. Use a teaspoon or a serrated edged knife to remove the seeds and the cores.

5. Cook the vegetables for about 2 minutes. Stir in the soy sauce and sesame oil and add the tomatoes. Heat through for 30 seconds and serve immediately.

TIME: Preparation takes about 25 minutes, cooking takes about 2-3 minutes.

VARIATION: Other vegetables such as broccoli florets, cauliflower florets, snow peas, zucchini or French beans may be used.

SERVING IDEA: Serve as a side dish or as a vegetarian main dish with plain or fried rice.

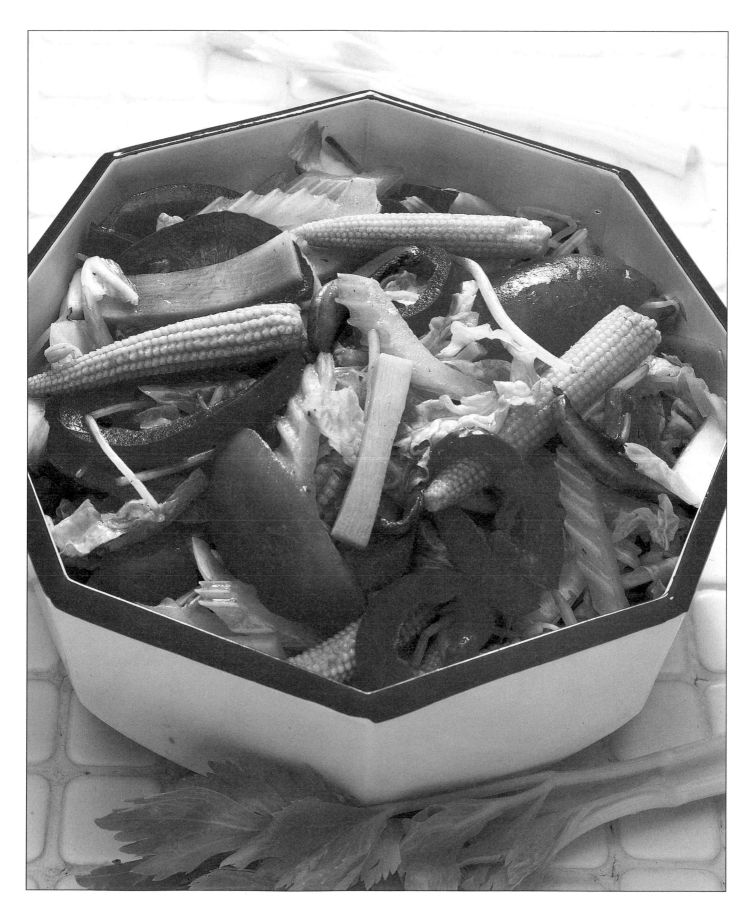

SWEET AND SOUR CABBAGE

A tasty combination which suits cabbage perfectly.

SERVES 4

1lb white cabbage, shredded
½ tsp baking soda
1 tsp salt
2 tsps sugar
1 tbsp oil

Sauce
2 tbsps sugar
2 tbsps wine vinegar
1 cup chicken stock or water
Pinch of salt
1 tbsp cornstarch
Few drops red food coloring
1 tsp tomato paste

1. Boil the cabbage in a large pan of water with the baking soda, salt and sugar for 2-3 minutes. Drain the cabbage and discard the boiling water.

2. Keep the cabbage in cold water for 5 minutes. Drain and keep on one side.

3. Heat the wok and add the oil. Fry the cabbage until it is heated through. Remove on to a serving dish.

4. Combine the sauce ingredients, stir well, add to the wok and gently bring to the boil, stirring. Stir over the heat until the sauce thickens. Pour over the cabbage and serve immediately.

TIME: Preparation takes 10 minutes, cooking takes 10 minutes.

COOK'S TIP: The red food coloring is optional as it only accentuates the color.

EGGPLANT AND PEPPERS SZECHUAN STYLE

Authentic Szechuan food is fiery hot. Outside China,
restaurants often tone down the taste for Western palates.

SERVES 4

1 large eggplant
⅓ cup oil
2 cloves garlic, crushed
1-inch piece fresh ginger, shredded
1 onion, cut into 1-inch pieces
1 small green pepper, seeded, cored and
    cut into 1-inch pieces
1 small red pepper, seeded, cored and cut
    into 1-inch pieces
1 red or green chili, seeded, cored and
    cut into thin strips
½ cup chicken or vegetable stock
1 tsp sugar
1 tsp vinegar
Pinch salt and pepper
1 tsp cornstarch
1 tbsp soy sauce
Dash sesame oil
Oil for cooking

1. Cut the eggplant in half and score the surface.

2. Sprinkle lightly with salt and leave to drain in a colander or on paper towels for 30 minutes.

3. After 30 minutes, squeeze the eggplant gently to extract any bitter juices and rinse thoroughly under cold water. Pat dry and cut the eggplant into 1-inch cubes.

4. Heat about 3 tbsps oil in a wok. Add the eggplant and stir-fry for about 4-5 minutes. It may be necessary to add more oil as the eggplant cooks. Remove from the wok and set aside.

5. Reheat the wok and add 2 tbsps oil. Add the garlic and ginger and stir-fry for 1 minute. Add the onion and stir-fry for 2 minutes. Add the green pepper, red pepper and chili pepper and stir-fry for 1 minute. Return the eggplant to the wok along with the remaining ingredients.

6. Bring to the boil, stirring constantly, and cook until the sauce thickens and clears. Serve immediately.

TIME: Preparation takes about 30 minutes, cooking takes about 7-8 minutes.

COOK'S TIP: Lightly salting the eggplant will help draw out any bitterness.

SERVING IDEA: Serve as a vegetarian stir-fry dish with plain or fried rice.

STIR-FRIED STICKY RICE

*Glutinous rice cooked with stir-fried mushrooms,
ginger and green onions.*

SERVES 4

9oz glutinous rice
2 tbsps oil
2 green onions, chopped
½ onion, chopped
1 slice fresh ginger root
4 dried Chinese black mushrooms, soaked
   for 15 minutes in warm water, drained
   and sliced
Salt and pepper

1. Wash the rice in plenty of cold water and place it in a sieve. Pour 5½ cups boiling water over the rice.

2. Heat the oil in a wok and fry the green onions, onion and ginger until golden brown.

3. Add the mushrooms and continue cooking, stirring and shaking the wok frequently.

4. Add the rice and stir well. Pour over enough water to cover the rice by ½ inch.

5. Cover and cook over a moderate heat until there is almost no liquid left. Reduce the heat and continue cooking until all the liquid has been absorbed. This takes approximately 20 minutes in total.

6. Add salt and pepper to taste, remove the slice of ginger, and serve immediately.

TIME: Preparation takes 5 minutes and cooking takes approximately 25 minutes.

VARIATION: Replace the water with beef stock to give the rice more flavor.

Microwave

Chicken Corn Chowder with Almonds
Shrimp and Lettuce Soup
Soup of Mushrooms and Peas
Shanghai Noodle Snack
Ham and Bean Fried Rice
Shrimp with Baby Corn
Scallops in Pepper Sauce
Beef with Green Pepper, Tomato
and Black Beans
Szechuan Beef
Singapore Chicken
Chicken with Snow Peas
Duck with Pineapple
Empress Chicken
Chicken with Hoisin Sauce and Cashews
Sweet-Sour Cabbage
Ten Varieties of Beauty
Beans with Bamboo Shoots

CHICKEN CORN CHOWDER WITH ALMONDS

Toasted almonds add a special flavor to this chowder.

SERVES 4

2 x 8oz cans creamed corn
1 quart chicken stock
2 chicken breasts, finely chopped
2 tbsps cornstarch
2 tbsps rice wine
½ cup toasted almonds
Salt and pepper

1. Combine corn, stock and chicken in a large deep bowl.

2. Partially cover and cook 3-5 minutes or until chicken is nearly cooked.

3. Combine cornstarch and rice wine and stir into the soup.

4. Cook 2-3 minutes to allow cornstarch thicken and clear.

5. Sprinkle with toasted almonds, season and serve.

TIME: Preparation takes 15 minutes, microwave cooking takes 5-8 minutes.

SHRIMP AND LETTUCE SOUP

*This unusual sounding recipe is wonderfully
tasty with its distinctly Chinese consistency.*

SERVES 4

4oz rice
1 quart hot chicken stock
1 piece fresh ginger root, grated
2 cups peeled, cooked shrimp
1 small head lettuce, shredded
Salt

1. Put the rice, stock and ginger into a large, deep bowl. Partially cover and cook 12 minutes on HIGH, stirring often.

2. Cook until the rice softens completely.

3. Add the shrimp, lettuce and salt. Leave the soup to stand, covered, for 5 minutes. Shrimp should heat through in the stock.

TIME: Preparation takes 10 minutes, microwave cooking takes 12 minutes plus 5 minutes standing time.

COOK'S TIP: Use your favorite lettuce in this soup.

SOUP OF MUSHROOMS AND PEAS

Astoundingly simple this recipe is the perfect answer to a soup in a hurry.

SERVES 4

12 dried Chinese mushrooms, soaked
   30 minutes
4oz ham, shredded
1 quart light stock
1 tbsp light soy sauce
1½ cups fresh peas
Salt and pepper

1. Remove the stems and slice the mushrooms finely.

2. Combine with the remaining ingredients and cook 10 minutes on HIGH or until peas are just tender.

TIME: Preparation takes 15 minutes, microwave cooking takes 10 minutes.

BUYING GUIDE: Chinese mushrooms are available in delicatessens and supermarkets.

SHANGHAI NOODLE SNACK

Crabmeat adds a touch of style to this tasty snack.

SERVES 6

1lb Chinese egg noodles
1 quart boiling water

Sauce
2 tbsps cornstarch dissolved in
   ¼ cup water
3 tbsps rice wine
1 tbsp light soy sauce
1¼ cups light stock
1 small piece ginger root, thinly sliced

4 green onions, thinly sliced diagonally
Meat from one large crab or 6oz frozen or
   canned crabmeat

1. Cook the noodles in the boiling water for 3 minutes on HIGH.

2. Leave to stand 5 minutes, covered, while preparing the sauce.

3. Combine the sauce ingredients in a deep bowl, stirring well to mix the cornstarch

4. Cook 2-3 minutes until the sauce thickens and clears.

5. Add the onions and crab and cook 3 seconds on HIGH.

6. Drain the noodles well and toss with the sauce to serve.

TIME: Preparation takes 15 minutes, microwave cooking takes 5-6 minutes plus 5 minutes standing time.

COOK'S TIP: Egg noodles are available in different thicknesses, choose the thicker variety for this dish.

HAM AND BEAN FRIED RICE

The perfect side dish or lunch time snack.

SERVE 4

3 tbsps oil
2 eggs, beaten
4oz ham, chopped
4 cups cooked rice
4oz green beans, cut in thin,
    diagonal slices
1 tbsp soy sauce
4 green onions, chopped
Salt and pepper

1. Heat a browning dish 5 minutes on HIGH.

2. Pour in half the oil and half the beaten egg and cook for 30 seconds on HIGH on one side.

3. Turn over and cook for 30 seconds on the second side.

4. Keep the egg warm and add the remaining oil to the dish.

5. Heat for 1 minute on HIGH and add the ham. Cover the dish and cook for 1 minute on HIGH.

6. Add the rice and cook, covered, for 5 minutes on HIGH.

7. Add the beans, soy sauce, onions and seasoning. Cook 1 minute on HIGH and toss the ingredients to mix well.

8. Slice the eggs into thin strips and scatter over the top of the rice. Cover the dish and leave to stand for 2 minutes before serving.

TIME: Preparation takes 15 minutes, microwave cooking takes 9 minutes plus 2 minutes standing time.

VARIATION: Substitute other vegetables such as mushrooms for the green beans.

SHRIMP WITH BABY CORN

*An old favorite which tastes great using
an up-to-date cooking method.*

SERVES 4

1½lbs shelled large shrimp, uncooked
3 tbsps oil
1 clove garlic, ground
1 small piece ginger root, minced
4 tbsps light stock
4 tbsps light soy sauce
4 tbsps rice wine
2 tsps cornstarch
2 tbsps Chinese parsley (cilantro
　　leaves)
2oz snow peas
4oz baby ears of corn
Salt

1. Heat a browning dish for 5 minutes on HIGH.

2. Shell and de-vein the shrimp if necessary. Add the oil to the dish and the shrimp.

3. Add the garlic and ginger and cook for 1-2 minutes on HIGH, stirring often.

4. Combine the stock, soy sauce, wine and cornstarch. Pour over the shrimp, and cook for 3-4 minutes on MEDIUM, stirring halfway through the cooking time.

5. Cut the stalks off the snow peas and add with the ears of corn to the dish. Cut the corn in half lengthwise if the ears are large. Cook for 1-2 minutes on MEDIUM, until the sauce thickens and clears.

6. If the shrimp are cooked after 3-4 minutes, remove them before adding the vegetables. Sprinkle with Chinese parsley before serving.

TIME: Preparation takes 20 minutes, microwave cooking takes 5-8 minutes.

SCALLOPS IN PEPPER SAUCE

Give your guests a treat with this special dish.

SERVES 4

1lb scallops, shelled and cleaned
½ clove garlic, finely chopped
3 tbsps rice wine
3 tbsps light soy sauce
Pinch sugar
Salt and pepper
1 tbsp cornstarch dissolved in
    ⅓ cup light stock
4 tbsps sweet chili sauce
1 small piece fresh ginger root, peeled and
    chopped
1 green pepper, thinly sliced
4 green onions, sliced or shredded

1. If the scallops are large, cut in half, horizontally. Place in a casserole dish with the garlic, wine, soy sauce, sugar, and salt and pepper.

2. Cover the dish and cook for 10 minutes on MEDIUM.

3. Remove the scallops and keep warm.

4. Add the cornstarch and stock to the hot liquid and stir well. Add the chili sauce and ginger root and cook 2-3 minutes, or until thickened.

5. Add the green pepper and onions to the sauce and return the scallops to the dish. Cook 1-2 minutes on HIGH, until the scallops are cooked and the vegetables are still crisp. Serve with rice.

TIME: Preparation takes 20 minutes, microwave cooking takes 13-15 minutes.

BEEF WITH GREEN PEPPER, TOMATO AND BLACK BEANS

Rump steak is needed for this recipe because of the quick cooking – cheaper cuts of meat would be too tough.

SERVES 4

1lb rump steak, cut into thin slices
4 tbsps soy sauce
2 tsps dry sherry or rice wine

Sauce
3 tbsps salted black beans
3 tbsps water
1¼ cups brown stock
1 tbsp sugar
3 tbsps cornstarch dissolved in the stock
1 clove garlic, finely ground
1 large green pepper, cut in 1-inch pieces

3 tomatoes, peeled and quartered
Salt and pepper

1. Mix the steak, soy sauce and wine and leave to marinate, covered, in the refrigerator for 30 minutes.

2. Crush the black beans and mix with the water. Leave to stand until ready to use.

3. Combine all the ingredients in a shallow dish, except for the pepper and tomatoes. Cover the dish and cook on HIGH 7-9 minutes, stirring halfway through the cooking time.

4. Once the sauce has cleared, add the pepper and tomatoes and cook 1 minute further on HIGH.

TIME: Preparation takes 30 minutes, microwave cooking takes 8-10 minutes.

SERVING IDEA: Serve this dish with plain rice and garnish with green onions.

SZECHUAN BEEF

This simple recipe brings out the flavor of the beef.

SERVES 4

1lb rump steak, shredded
2 tbsps oil
½ dried chili pepper, crushed
4 tbsps soy sauce
½ cup stock
2 tbsps cornstarch
3 sticks celery, shredded
1 sweet red pepper, shredded

1. Heat a browning dish for 5 minutes on HIGH.

2. Combine meat and oil and add to the dish. Cook 2 minutes on HIGH in 2 or 3 batches. Re-heat browning dish 2 minutes after each batch.

3. Add the crushed chili pepper.

4. Mix the soy sauce and stock and gradually stir into the cornstarch. Pour over the steak and cook 2-3 minutes.

5. Add the celery and red pepper and mix together with the meat and sauce.

6. Cook a further 1 minute on HIGH until the sauce has thickened but the vegetables are still crisp.

TIME: Preparation takes 20 minutes, microwave cooking takes 6-18 minutes.

COOK'S TIP: Do not substitute a cheaper cut of meat or the final result will be Tough Beef!

SINGAPORE CHICKEN

Chicken, pineapple and mandarin
form the basis of this colorful dish.

SERVES 4

2 tbsps oil
2 tsps curry powder
1lb chicken, skinned, boned and cut
   into bite-sized pieces
1 large onion, cut in large pieces
1 tbsp cornstarch
8oz can pineapple chunks, juice
   reserved
10oz can mandarin orange segments,
   juice reserved
1 cup bean sprouts
Dash soy sauce
Salt and pepper

1. Heat the oil in a large casserole dish for 30 seconds on HIGH.

2. Add the curry powder, and cook 30 seconds on HIGH.

3. Add the chicken, cover the dish and cook 5 minutes on HIGH.

4. Add the onion, mix the cornstarch with the reserved pineapple and orange juice and add to the chicken. Cover and cook 5 minutes on HIGH, stirring occasionally after 1 minute.

5. When the sauce thickens, add the pineapple, orange segments and bean sprouts.

6. Leave to stand 2 minutes before serving. Serve with fried or plain boiled rice.

TIME: Preparation takes 20 minutes, microwave cooking takes 11 minutes
plus 2 minutes standing time.

COOK'S TIP: Do not buy the bean sprouts too far in advance as they deteriorate rapidly.

CHICKEN WITH SNOW PEAS

Snow peas bring a flavor all their own to any recipe.

SERVES 4

2 tbsps oil
1lb chicken breasts, skinned, boned and
   cut into thin slivers
2 tsps cornstarch
3 tbsps rice wine
3 tbsps light soy sauce
2 tbsps oyster sauce
4 tbsps chicken stock
Dash sesame oil
Salt and pepper
4oz snow peas

1. Heat the oil 30 seconds on HIGH in a large casserole dish.

2. Mix the remaining ingredients except the snow peas, and pour over the chicken.

3. Cover and cook 7-9 minutes on HIGH, stirring halfway through cooking time.

4. Add the snow peas, re-cover the dish and cook 30 seconds on HIGH.

5. Leave to stand for 2 minutes before serving. Serve with rice.

TIME: Preparation takes 20 minutes, microwave cooking takes 8½-9½ minutes plus 2 minutes standing time.

BUYING GUIDE: Oyster sauce is a common ingredient in Chinese cooking and is widely available in supermarkets.

DUCK WITH PINEAPPLE

A great combination that always goes down well.

SERVES 4

Sauce
8oz can crushed pineapple, or
   1 fresh pineapple, peeled and cored
1½ tsps cornstarch dissolved in
   1 tbsp water
1 tbsp light soy sauce
1½ tsps sugar
1 tbsp white wine
1 piece ginger root, grated
Pinch salt

5lb duckling
2 tbsps oil
2 tbsps soy sauce

Garnish
4 chives, shredded

1. If using fresh pineapple, work in a food processor until finely chopped. Add remaining sauce ingredients and mix well in a small, deep bowl. Cook 4 minutes on HIGH until the sauce thickens and clears.

2. Skin the duck and remove the leg and breast meat. Cut into thin slivers.

3. Heat a browning dish 5 minutes on HIGH. Toss the oil and duck together, and add to the browning dish. Cook, uncovered, 4 minutes on HIGH.

4. Add the soy sauce, cover the dish and reduce the setting to MEDIUM. Cook a further 3 minutes or until duck is tender.

5. Remove duck to a serving dish and keep warm. Coat with the pineapple sauce and sprinkle on the chives. Serve with rice.

TIME: Preparation takes 20 minutes, microwave cooking takes 9-10 minutes.

EMPRESS CHICKEN

As its name suggests this is a special dish fit for any guest.

SERVES 4

---

4 chicken wings
4 chicken breasts, skinned
12 dried Chinese mushrooms
½ cup soy sauce
2½ cups chicken stock mixed with
    3 tbsps cornstarch
1 tbsp sugar
2 pieces star anise
2 slices ginger root
1 tbsp rice wine
½ tsp salt
2 cans bamboo shoots, drained and cut in
    strips if thick
4 green onions, sliced

---

1. With a heavy clever, chop the chicken, through the bones, into large chunks. Remove any splinters of bone.

2. Soak the mushrooms in hot water for 30 minutes. Drain and trim off the stems.

3. Put the chicken, mushrooms and remaining ingredients, except the onions and bamboo shoots, into a deep casserole.

4. Cover well and cook 15 minutes on HIGH or until the chicken is completely cooked.

5. Add the bamboo shoots and sliced onions. Leave to stand 3 minutes and remove star anise before serving.

TIME: Preparation takes 30 minutes, microwave cooking takes 15 minutes plus 3 minutes standing time.

COOK'S TIP: Dried Chinese mushrooms have a very distinctive flavor so only substitute fresh mushrooms as a last resort.

CHICKEN WITH HOISIN SAUCE AND CASHEWS

*Cashews accentuate the taste of meat
while adding a delightful flavor.*

SERVES 4

1lb chicken, skinned, boned and cut
    into bite-sized pieces
1 tbsp cornstarch
1¼ cups stock
1 tbsp light soy sauce
1 clove garlic, finely minced
1 tbsp white wine
4 tbsps Hoisin sauce
2oz roasted cashew nuts
4 green onions, diagonally sliced

1. Combine the chicken with all the
ingredients except the nuts and onions.

2. Put into a casserole dish, cover and
cook on HIGH for 7-9 minutes, stirring
halfway through the cooking time.

3. Once the sauce has thickened and the
cornstarch has cleared, add the nuts and
the green onions.

4. Re-cover the dish and leave to stand 2
minutes before serving. Serve with rice.

TIME: Preparation takes 20 minutes, microwave cooking takes 7-9 minutes
plus 2 minutes standing time.

COOK'S TIP: Ensure the cashew nuts are unsalted. If you can only
buy salted ones, rinse before using.

SWEET-SOUR CABBAGE

The perfect refreshing side dish.

SERVES 4

---

1 medium head white cabbage,
    about 2lbs
1 small red chili pepper (use less if
    desired)
½ cup light brown sugar
⅓ cup rice wine vinegar
2 tbsps light soy sauce
Salt
3 tbsps oil

---

1. Cut the cabbage into ½-inch slices, discarding the core. Cut the chili pepper into thin, short strips, discarding the seeds.

2. Mix all the ingredients together except the oil.

3. Pour the oil into a large bowl and heat for 2 minutes on HIGH.

4. Add the cabbage and the liquid and cover the bowl with pierced plastic wrap. Cook on HIGH for 9-11 minutes.

5. Allow to cool in the bowl, stirring frequently. When cold, refrigerate.

TIME: Preparation takes 20 minutes, microwave cooking takes 11-13 minutes.

COOK'S TIP: Vary the amount of sugar and chili pepper according to your own taste.

TEN VARIETIES OF BEAUTY

The name of this recipe refers to the variety
of vegetables in the recipe.

SERVES 4-6

4 tbsps oil
3 sticks celery, diagonally sliced
2 carrots, peeled and cut into ribbons with
    a vegetable peeler
3oz snow peas
1 red pepper, thickly sliced
8 ears of baby corn
4 green onions, diagonally sliced
1 cup bean sprouts
10 water chestnuts, sliced
½ small can sliced bamboo shoots
10 Chinese dried mushrooms, soaked in
    hot water, stalks removed
1¼ cups chicken stock
2 tbsps cornstarch
3 tbsps light soy sauce
Sesame oil

1. Heat a browning dish for 5 minutes on
HIGH. Pour in the oil and add the celery
and carrots. Cook for 1 minute on HIGH.

2. Remove from the dish and add the
snow peas, red pepper and corn. Cook for
1 minute on HIGH and place with the
celery and carrots.

3. Add the onions, bean sprouts, water
chestnuts and bamboo shoots to the dish.
Cook for 1 minute on HIGH, adding the
mushrooms after 30 seconds.

4. Place with the rest of vegetables.

5. Combine the rest of the ingredients in a
glass measure. Cook 2-3 minutes on HIGH
until thickened. Taste and add salt if
necessary. Pour over the vegetables and
stir carefully.

6. Reheat for 1-2 minutes on HIGH before
serving.

TIME: Preparation takes 20 minutes, microwave cooking takes 6-8 minutes.

BEANS WITH BAMBOO SHOOTS

An unusual combination which is wonderfully tasty.

SERVES 4

6 pieces Chinese black fungi (tree or wood
    ears), soaked 30 minutes
8oz green beans, cut into 2 inch diagonal
    pieces
2 whole pieces canned bamboo shoots,
    cut into thin triangular pieces
2 tbsps oil
2 tbsps soy sauce
2 tsps cornstarch
4 tbsps light stock and wine mixed
Dash sesame oil
Salt and pepper

1. Heat a browning dish for 5 minutes on HIGH. Pour in the oil and add the beans and bamboo shoots. Cook, uncovered, for 2 minutes on HIGH.

2. Add the tree ears, cover the dish and leave to stand while preparing the sauce.

3. Mix the remaining ingredients except the sesame oil in a glass measure. Cook for 2 minutes on HIGH, stirring once until thickened.

4. Combine with the vegetables and stir in the sesame oil to serve.

TIME: Preparation takes 30 minutes, microwave cooking takes 4 minutes.

Desserts

Almond Float with Fruit
Kiwi and Coconut Duo
Spun Fruits
Peking Toffee Apples
Almond Cookies
Melon Salad
Exotic Fruit Salad
Sweet Bean Wontons
Half-Moon Banana Pastries

ALMOND FLOAT WITH FRUIT

Sweet dishes are not often served in the course of a Chinese meal. Banquets are the exception, and this elegant fruit salad is certainly special enough.

SERVES 6-8

1 envelope unflavored gelatin
⅓ cup cold water
⅓ cup sugar
1¼ cups milk
1 tsp almond extract
Few drops red or yellow food coloring
 (optional)

Almond Sugar Syrup
⅓ cup sugar
2½ cups water
½ tsp almond extract
Fresh fruit such as kiwi, mango,
 pineapple, bananas, litchis, oranges or
 satsumas, peaches, berries, cherries,
 grapes or starfruit
Fresh mint for garnish

1. Allow the gelatin to soften in the cold water for about 10 minutes or until spongy. Put in a large mixing bowl.

2. Bring ¾ cup water to the boil and stir in the sugar. Pour into the gelatin and water mixture and stir until gelatin and sugar dissolves.

3. Add milk, 1 tsp almond essence and food coloring if using. Mix well and pour into a 8-inch square pan. Chill in the refrigerator until set.

4. Mix the sugar and water for the syrup together in a heavy-based pan. Cook over gentle heat until the sugar dissolves. Bring to the boil and allow to boil for about 2 minutes, or until the syrup thickens slightly. Add the almond essence and allow to cool at room temperature. Chill in the refrigerator until ready to use.

5. Prepare the fruit and place in attractive serving dish. Pour over the chilled syrup and mix well.

6. Cut the set almond float into 1 inch diamond shapes or cubes. Use a spatula to remove them from the pan and stir them gently into the fruit mixture. Decorate with sprigs of fresh mint to serve.

TIME: Preparation takes about 25 minutes. The almond float will need about 2 hours to set.

PREPARATION: To prepare kiwi fruit, peel with a swivel vegetable peeler and cut into thin rounds. To prepare litchis, peel and cut into thin slices around the large stone. To prepare starfruit, wash and cut crosswise into thin slices.

BUYING GUIDE: Use whatever fruits are in season at the moment, or use good quality canned fruit. Exotic fruits are avilable in most large supermarkets. Allow about 2lbs of fruit for 6-8 people.

KIWI AND COCONUT DUO

*Incredibly simple to prepare, this recipe is a delicious
blend of kiwi fruit, fresh coconut and coconut milk.*

SERVES 4

4 kiwi fruit
1 fresh coconut
A little sugar (optional)

1. Remove the stalks from the ends of the kiwis.

2. Peel them lengthwise with a small sharp knife.

3. Slice them thinly widthways.

4. Cut the coconut into pieces, reserving all the milk.

5. Cut the coconut flesh into very thin slices.

6. Arrange the kiwi slices on a serving plate and surround with the slices of coconut.

7. Add a little sugar to the coconut milk if desired and pour over the fruit. Serve chilled.

TIME: Preparation takes about 25 minutes.

VARIATION: Coconut milk can now be bought in cans. It is usually of very high quality and is thicker than fresh coconut milk.

COOK'S TIP: The addition of sugar to the milk is optional, and depends upon the acidity of the milk.

SPUN FRUITS

*Often called toffee fruits, this dessert consists of fruit
fried in batter and coated with a thin, crisp caramel glaze.*

SERVES 4

Batter
1 cup all-purpose flour, sifted
Pinch salt
1 egg
½ cup water and milk mixed half and half
Oil for deep frying

Caramel Syrup
1 cup sugar
3 tbsps water
1 tbsp oil

1 large apple, peeled, cored and cut into
  2-inch chunks
1 banana, peeled and cut into 1-inch pieces
Ice water

1. To prepare the batter, combine all the batter ingredients, except the oil for deep frying, in a liquidizer or food processor and process to blend. Pour into a bowl and dip in the prepared fruit.

2. In a heavy-based saucepan, combine the sugar with the water and oil and cook over very low heat until the sugar dissolves. Bring to the boil and allow to cook rapidly until a pale caramel color.

3. While the sugar is dissolving heat the oil in a wok and fry the batter-dipped fruit, a few pieces at a time.

4. While the fruit is still hot and crisp use chopsticks or a pair of tongs to dip the fruit into the hot caramel syrups. Stir each piece around to coat evenly.

5. Dip immediately into ice water to harden the syrup and place each piece on a greased dish. Continue cooking all the fruit in the same way.

6. Once the caramel has hardened and the fruit has cooled, transfer to a clean serving plate.

TIME: Preparation takes about 25 minutes, cooking takes from 10-15 minutes.

VARIATION: Litchis may be used. Organization is very important for the success of this dish. Have the batter ready, syrup prepared, fruit sliced and ice water on hand before beginning.

WATCHPOINT: Watch the syrup carefully and do not allow it to become too brown. This will give a bitter taste to the dish.

PEKING TOFFEE APPLES

A quick and easy dessert to prepare and one which you never tire of!

SERVES 4

---

4 crisp apples
1 egg
½ cup flour
Oil for deep frying
⅓ cup sugar
3 tbsps oil
3 tbsps syrup

---

1. Peel, core and thickly slice the apples.

2. Blend the egg, flour and ¼ cup water to make a smooth batter.

3. Dip each piece of apple in the batter.

4. Deep fry the apple in the oil for 2-3 minutes. Drain.

5. Heat the sugar, oil and 2 tbsps water in a pan over a low heat for 5 minutes.

6. Add the syrup, and stir for a further 2 minutes.

7. Add the apple pieces and stir slowly, covering each piece of apple with syrup.

8. Quickly spoon hot, syrup-covered apples into a large bowl of iced water to harden syrup. Remove quickly and serve.

TIME: Preparation takes 10 minutes, cooking takes 10 minutes.

ALMOND COOKIES

In China these cookies are often eaten as a between-meal snack. In Western-style cuisine, they make a good accompaniment to fruit or sherbet.

MAKES 30 COOKIES

½ cup butter or margarine
4 tbsps superfine sugar
2 tbsps light brown sugar
1 egg, beaten
Almond extract
1 cup all-purpose flour
1 tsp baking powder
Pinch salt
1oz ground almonds, blanched or
    unblanched
2 tbsps water
30 whole blanched almonds

1. Cream the butter or margarine together with the two sugars until light and fluffy.

2. Divide the beaten egg in half and add half to the sugar mixture with a few drops of the almond essence and beat until smooth. Reserve the remaining egg for later use. Sift the flour, baking powder and salt into the egg mixture and add the ground almonds. Stir well by hand.

3. Shape the mixture into small balls and place well apart on a lightly greased cookie sheet. Flatten slightly and press an almond on to the top of each one.

4. Mix the reserved egg with the water and brush each cookie before baking.

5. Place in a preheated 350°F oven and bake for 12-15 minutes. Cookies will be a pale golden color when done.

TIME: Preparation takes about 10 minutes. If the dough becomes too soft, refrigerate for 10 minutes before shaping. Cooking takes about 12-15 minutes per batch.

COOK'S TIP: Roll the mixture on a floured surface with floured hands to prevent sticking.

WATCHPOINT: Do not over beat once the almonds are added. They will begin to oil and the mixture will become too soft and sticky to shape.

SERVING IDEA: Serve with fruit, ice cream or sherbet.

FREEZING: Cookies may be frozen baked or unbaked. Defrost uncooked dough completely at room temperature before baking. Baked cookies may be re-crisped by heating in the oven for about 2 minutes and then allowed to cool before serving.

MELON SALAD

*A refreshing fruit salad, which is especially tasty
served after a heavy meal of many courses.*

SERVES 4

---

1 large cantaloupe melon
1 mango
4 canned litchis
4 large or 8 small strawberries
Litchi syrup from the can

---

1. Peel and seed the melon and cut into thin slices.

2. Peel and pit the mango and cut into thin slices.

3. Using a melon baller, cut as many balls as possible out the strawberries.

4. Arrange the melon slices evenly on 4 small plates.

5. Spread a layer of mango over the melon. Place a litchi in the center of each plate and arrange a few strawberry balls around the edges.

6. Divide the litchi syrup evenly between the plates of fruit and chill them in the refrigerator before serving.

TIME: Preparation takes about 30 minutes.

VARIATION: Use a honeydew melon instead of the cantaloupe variety.

COOK'S TIP: This dessert is best served well chilled from the refrigerator, so prepare it several hours in advance of serving.

EXOTIC FRUIT SALAD

Fresh fruit marinated in orange and litchi juice with just a hint of almond.

SERVES 4

1 papaya
1 pomegranate
2 kiwi fruit
4 rambutan fruit
4 canned litchis, plus the juice from the can
3 blood oranges
3 drops bitter almond extract, or ordinary
   almond extract

1. Peel all the fruit except the oranges, removing pips or pitting each fruit as necessary. Try to buy a fully ripe papaya for the salad. Cut it in half. Using a small spoon, remove all the pips and any stringy skin around them. Peel each half, but not too thickly as the flesh immediately below the skin is very good. Finally, cut the flesh into thin slices or other fancy shapes.

2. Peel two of the oranges. Remove all the pith and cut the flesh into small pieces.

3. Squeeze the juice from the remaining orange, mix this with the canned litchi juice and add the almond extract.

4. Cut all the remaining fruit into slices, rounds or small cubes and combine these with the prepared papaya and oranges in a bowl. Pour over the almond flavored juices and leave the salad to marinate for a few hours in the refrigerator.

5. Serve chilled.

TIME: Preparation takes about 1 hour and the salad should be left to marinate for at least 3 hours.

SERVING IDEA: Cut a few fresh mint leaves into thin strips to garnish the fruit salad just before serving.

WATCHPOINT: Exotic fruit often arrives in the ships before it is ripe. The solution is to sweeten the sauce slightly before marinating the fruit in order to eliminate acidity.

BUYING GUIDE: If any of the fruits are out of season and unavailable, substitute other appropriate fruit, as desired.

SWEET BEAN WONTONS

*Wonton snacks, either sweet or savory, are another popular
tea house treat. Made from prepared wonton wrappers and
ready-made bean paste, they couldn't be more simple.*

SERVES 6

15 wonton wrappers
8oz sweet red bean paste
1 tbsp cornstarch
4 tbsps cold water
Oil for deep frying
Honey

1. Take wonton wrapper in the palm of your hand and place a little of the red bean paste slightly above the center.

2. Mix together the cornstarch and water and moisten the edge around the filling.

3. Fold over, slightly off center.

4. Pull the sides together, using the cornstarch and water paste to stick the two together.

5. Turn inside out by gently pushing the filled center.

6. Heat enough oil in a wok for deep-fat frying and when hot, put in 4 of the filled wontons at a time. Cook until crisp and golden and remove to paper towels to drain. Repeat with the remaining filled wontons. Served drizzled with honey.

VARIATION: Add a small amount of grated ginger to the red bean paste for a slight change in flavor. Wontons may also be sprinkled with sugar instead of honey.

BUYING GUIDE: Wontons, wonton wrappers and red bean paste are available in Chinese supermarkets.

HALF-MOON BANANA PASTRIES

*These crunchy pastries are rather dry, and are
traditionally served with a cup of Chinese tea.*

SERVES 4

Dough
½ cup margarine
1lb all-purpose flour, sifted
Pinch salt
½ cup water

Filling
3 bananas
2 tsps sugar
Pinch cinnamon
Few drops of lemon juice
1 egg yolk, beaten

1. Cut the margarine into the flour and salt. Using your fingers, incorporate the water gradually to form a ball. Wrap a damp cloth around the dough and leave it to rest in a cool place for 30 minutes.

2. Peel and crush the bananas with a fork. Add the sugar, cinnamon and lemon juice. Mix together well.

3. Roll out small pieces of dough on a lightly floured surface and cut into circles. Place a little of the banana filling on each round of dough. Fold into half-moon shapes and seal the edges first by pinching together with your fingers and then by decorating with a fork.

4. Continue until all the dough and filling have been used.

5. Brush the beaten egg yolk over the half-moon pastries. Pierce the pastries once to allow steam to escape during cooking. Cook in a moderate oven, 350°F, for approximately 20 minutes, until crisp and golden.

TIME: Preparation takes about 25 minutes, resting time for the dough is 30 minutes and cooking takes approximately 20 minutes.

VARIATION: Make up the pastries using different fruit fillings.

COOK'S TIP: The cooked dough in this recipe is very crisp. Serve the pastries with a fruit drink in summer and hot Chinese tea in winter.

WATCHPOINT: Be sure to seal the edges of the pastries thoroughly so that no filling escapes during cooking.

Glossary

Bean Pastes

Sauces made from soya beans. There are many varieties of bean paste. Hot bean paste is made with chillies and is salty. Soy Bean Paste is dark in color, very salty and is made with fermented soya beans. Sweet Bean Paste is made with black soya beans, sugar, flour and spices. Yellow Bean Paste is made with yellow soya beans, and is also quite salty in taste.

Bean Sprouts

These are the shoots of mung beans or soya beans. They are readily available from most supermarkets. Although beans sprouts will keep for about a day in a perforated plastic bag it is best to buy them on the day of use.

Black Bean Sauce

This can be bought ready-made from shops or made with 3-4 tbsps steamed black soya beans mixed to a paste with 2 tbsps oil and 2 tbsps sugar.

Chili Sauce

This is a very hot and tangy sauce made from chilies and vinegar. Chili sauce can be easily purchased from many supermarkets and all Chinese grocers. It is used to give extra flavor to a wide variety of savory Chinese dishes.

Chilies

There are numerous varieties of chillies varying in size and strength of flavor. Commonly used in Eastern cooking are the red and green finger-like chilies about 4-inches long, and the tiny red and green bird's eye chilies which are extremely hot.
When preparing chilies it is advisable to wear rubber gloves and avoid getting the oils near lips or eyes. The seeds, which are very hot, should be discarded unless a fiery dish is required.

Chinese Cabbage

There are two main varieties, Pak-choy and Choy-sum. These are sometimes available in supermarkets and vegetable markets as well as Chinese grocers. Chinese leaves, on the other hand, are available in most supermarkets. All these cabbages can be substituted by ordinary cabbage.

Chinese Parsley

Otherwise known as fresh cilantro, this is a herb of Indian origin, which is used as a flavoring and a garnish. The flat leaves have a strong flavor and cannot be substituted by Western parsley.

Chinese Wine

There are many kinds of wine made from rice, Shao Hsing and Japanese Sake are two of the most popular and one can be substituted for the other. If you cannot obtain either of these, dry sherry is a good substitute.

Cloud Ear

This is known by many names e.g. wood ear, snow fungus, sea jelly or jelly sheet. It is actually a dried fungus which when soaked in water, resembles a puffed ear, hence the name. It has no flavor and is used only to add texture to a dish. They are available in Chinese grocers.

Cooked Oil

This is oil which has been used at least once before and therefore has a richer flavor than new cooking oil. If you wish to use new oil, heat it until it smokes before using.

Five-Spice Powder

This is a blend of cinnamon, cloves, star anise, fennel and brown peppercorns. The mixture is often used to marinate meat or poultry.

Ginger

The root stem of this plant can be purchased whole, sliced or ground, but it is always best to use fresh ginger and chop or grate as needed. Ginger is a vital ingredient in Chinese cooking as nearly all traditional meat and fish dishes use root ginger.

Hoisin Sauce

This is a brownish-red sauce made from soya beans, salt, chili, sugar, garlic, vinegar and flour. It has a sweet, tangy flavor and can be bought from Chinese or large supermarkets. It is used in cooking as well as being served as a dip for meats, etc.

Maltose

A molasses-like substance which is made by fermenting barley or a similar grain. It can be substituted in recipes by honey or corn syrup.

Monosodium Glutamate

This is a white crytalline substance used extensively in Chinese cooking for tenderizing meat and enhancing the flavor of dishes. It should be used sparingly as too much will spoil the dish. It can be totally omitted without unduly altering the taste of a dish.

Dried Mushrooms

Tree Fungus found in the East on oak logs and Shii trees. They are sold dried and have to be reconstituted by soaking in hot water. They are expensive, but only a few are needed to impart their distinctive woody flavor to a dish.

Noodles

There are many different kinds of noodles. Some are made from wheat flour, some from rice flour and some from bean flour. Egg noodles can be either thin or thick. The thin noodles are sold in "cakes" whereas the thick noodles are spaghetti-like and are often called Shanghai noodles. Bean Thread noodles are thin, white noodles which go transparent when cooked. They are mostly used in soups and stews and should be soaked before use. Rice Stick noodles are very thin noodles.

Oyster Sauce

This is a special sauce produced from soy sauce and oysters which have been fermented together. It is now widely available in supermarkets.

Rice

There are many different varieties of rice. Long-grained rice is the variety usually used for making simple rice dishes. Basmati is the finest and most expensive long-grain rice. Glutinous rice is also common in Chinese cooking. It is a medium-grain rice used for making puddings and savory dishes.

Sesame Oil

An aromatic oil produced from sesame seeds. This has a special flavor and is used as a seasoning and is a vital ingredient in some sauces. It is available from most supermarkets.

Soy Sauce

There are two different types; one is

dark and the other is light. Both are used for flavoring nearly all Chinese foods. The dark soy sauce is stronger in flavor and thicker, while the light soy sauce is a weaker infusion.

Star Anise

This is an eight-pointed clove with a strong anise smell and flavor. It can be purchased as a powder or whole.

Szechuan Pickle

This salty pickle is made from cabbage, chilies and mustard and has a strong flavor. It is sold in jars and cans and is available from Chinese supermarkets.

Water Chestnuts

These are the bulb-like stems of the bulrush. They are slightly sweet and have a crisp texture.

Index